THE DARK KNIGHT
DEVOTIONALS

THE DARK KNIGHT
DEVOTIONALS

Finding Biblical Truth in the World of Batman

Daniel V. Debs

ELM HILL

A Division of
HarperCollins Christian Publishing

www.elmhillbooks.com

The Dark Knight Devotionals
Finding Biblical Truth in the World of Batman

Published in Nashville, Tennessee, by Elm Hill, an imprint of Thomas Nelson. Elm Hill and Thomas Nelson are registered trademarks of HarperCollins Christian Publishing, Inc.

Publisher's Note: The sole purpose of this work is to present a study and analysis of the biblical parallels of Christian values found by the author in the Batman stories. This work does not intend to replicate or recreate any part of the story in any of the Batman series.

Elm Hill titles may be purchased in bulk for educational, business, fund-raising, or sales promotional use. For information, please e-mail SpecialMarkets@ ThomasNelson.com.

Library of Congress Cataloging-in-Publication Data

Library of Congress Control Number: 2018958987

ISBN 978-1-595558657 (Paperback)
ISBN 978-1-595558633 (eBook)

ACKNOWLEDGMENTS

To my wife Teairra, thank you for your constant encouragement and prayers!

To Mom and Dad and my brother Steve for their love and support.

To my cousins, Thom and Jenn, who provided valuable feedback and prayers throughout this project, thank you!

To Bob Kane and Bill Finger for creating one of the most enduring fictional characters of our time.

Finally and most importantly, thank you to God for saving us all through Jesus Christ, the greatest Hero in the history of the universe...

CONTENTS

INTRODUCTION

Heroes – our culture, as well as the many ancient cultures that have preceded us, has been enamored with tales of heroic acts and mighty figures who perform them. From the Greek gods to classic literature, human beings seemingly have an intrinsic desire to save and to be saved. This has only continued in our day and age. Since before World War II, the most recurring genre of heroic fiction has been superhero comic books. Superheroes have permeated our popular culture for several decades, the last fifteen years or so in particular. One character especially has always been at the forefront – Bruce Wayne, the Batman.

Debuting in 1939, Batman was created by Bob Kane and Bill Finger. The famous backstory goes like this. Bruce Wayne, son of wealthy Gotham surgeon Thomas Wayne and Martha Wayne, witnesses his parents' murder in front of him by a man with a gun. Devastated and traumatized, Bruce dedicates his life to avenging his parents and preventing similar tragedies from harming anyone else. After traveling around the world and honing his body and mind, Bruce concocts the Batman, a new persona through whom he can traverse Gotham's underworld and help rid the city of the evil that took his parents' lives.

Superheroes and comic books don't seem like the place you'd find parallels of Christian values. True, comics like most media in this world, can be full of glorified sin. They can be sexually suggestive or perverse, portray too much violence, or lead impressionable readers down the wrong path. But there are also surprisingly poignant lessons to be found in various stories, some built on the same universal truths found in the Bible.

Even when it is unintentional on the creators' parts, a superhero comic can't help but reflect in some way, the ultimate Hero, if the title characters are indeed doing good deeds. True heroism was defined when God came to earth in the form of His Son and He took the punishment for our sins in order to save us. Jesus performed the greatest heroic act the universe will ever see and saved countless souls from perdition. He did this out of great love for us all.

Batman is a character that, as previously mentioned, has been around for decades. He has been handled by numerous writers and artists in different media. While the character has sometimes been portrayed as a crazy person only motivated by revenge (he does dress up as a bat after all; irrational behavior in the real world), in most stories Bruce Wayne is just a man trying to save the city he loves, a place incapable of saving itself. What is the driving motivation then? Love, for Gotham and its people, his friends and to honor his parents' memory.

Jesus says this in John 15:13 (ESV), "Greater love has no one than this, that someone lay down his life for his friends."

In a small way, we see this attitude reflected in many Batman stories, a willingness to sacrifice himself to save others. If it takes his life to save someone else, he will risk it. One example is found in *The Dark Knight*, a film this devotional will explore in further detail. Batman sacrifices his reputation in order to give Gotham a chance against corruption and evil. Another instance is found in *The Dark Knight Rises*. Batman is preparing to save his city from Bane, a masked terrorist, when Catwoman beseeches him to reconsider.

"You don't owe these people anymore," she says, referring to Gotham City. "You've given them everything."

Batman looks at her stoically. "Not everything. Not yet." In that moment, he knows he could die but it's worth it to save his city. Bruce

Wayne's entire life reflects John 15:13. What he really wanted for his life was unimportant as long as Gotham needed saving.

There are lines also that Batman won't cross. He gruffly tells Catwoman, "No guns; no killing!" when she tries to fire at one of Bane's cronies. In the comic entitled *Batman: Vengeance of Bane*, which is the villain's debut, Bane confronts Batman for the first time and is perplexed. Witnessing Batman save a burglar from falling off a rooftop, Bane says, "You do not kill. That is strange. A creature cloaked in nightmare. A figure of terror in a city of terror. And yet you will not break the Sixth Commandment." Batman won't take a life nor will he allow one to be taken.

Of course, Batman is still just a mortal. He isn't perfect, far from it. Many stories also depict him as having tunnel vision or being obsessive. He makes mistakes, just as we all do. Those too can be learning experiences for the reader. In the end, Bruce Wayne needs to be saved as well. The only One who can truly save us is Jesus Christ.

So let's take a stroll through the mean streets of Gotham City and see how the adventures of the Dark Knight can point us towards our Ultimate Hero.

Batman

GOTHAM CITY

A story is often only as good as its setting and perhaps there is no better example of this than in Batman. A character like him could only exist in a place such as Gotham City, a representation of civilization at its ugliest. Often depicted as an urban nightmare, Gotham is a place full of corruption, despair, and anguish. To put it simply, it's a tough place to live. In the afterword of the novel *Batman: Knightfall*, legendary comic writer Dennis O'Neil referred to Gotham City as being akin to "Manhattan below 14th street at eleven minutes past midnight on the coldest night in November."

One of the most memorable depictions of Gotham is seen in Tim Burton's *Batman*, released in the summer of 1989. A landmark film in many ways, the portrayal of Gotham as a complicated urban landscape filled with back alleys, gothic architecture, and enormous statues has influenced many subsequent comics, TV shows, and movies since. The opening shot of the film is a wide angle view of the island in its entirety, a dense and sprawling concrete jungle, which somehow still seems pitch black in spite of the numerous lights across the skyline.

However, much like how a person's personality isn't determined by their outward appearance, Gotham's intimidating atmosphere stems from its soul. Rotten to its core, Gotham's citizens live in constant fear of criminals and evildoers. Corruption flows throughout; crooked cops are everywhere, the politicians live off the fat of the land, and ordinary people are preyed upon. It's no wonder this place needs a hero like Batman.

Continuing after that opening scene, a family of three are trying to make their way home. Unable to get a cab, which in this city is a lifeline, they're forced to walk. Wading through the seedy elements, they're cornered in an alley by a pair of pickpockets. They club the father over the head and steal their money, leaving the mother and son to fend for themselves. Later in the film, the Joker is riding through the city on a parade float, shooting cash bills into the air. People are going ballistic, scrambling to grab as much of the money as they can. Gotham is truly a depraved place at times.

It can be easy to watch the movie or read any Batman comic and brush this off as a ridiculous, over the top comic book fantasy. But without the guiding principles of God, this is what humanity looks like. Think of what kind of evil was running rampant prior to the Flood. Things were so bad that God had to drown out the entire planet to put a stop to the evil behavior (Genesis 6-7). Elsewhere in Genesis is the story of Sodom and Gomorrah, two cities so wicked that God smoked them from the face of the earth. Genesis 19:24-25 (ESV) says, "Then the Lord rained on Sodom and Gomorrah sulfur and fire from the Lord out of heaven. And He overthrew those cities, and all the valley, and all the inhabitants of the cities, and what grew on the ground." These were cities ruled by Satan's way of life, which is sinful and leads to death. It is a perversion of God's intentions. Prior to blowing the two cities away, God had sent two angels ahead of Him to rescue Lot and his family. A huge crowd of people came out of the city gates and confronted Lot and the two visitors (they didn't realize these men were actually angels). The crowd demanded that Lot bring the two men outside so that they could meet them. The New King James version says in Genesis 19:5, "Bring them out to us that we may know them carnally." What this really means is the crowd wanted to have sex with them. Clearly, this was a breaking point. The angels get Lot and his family to safety and then God finally brings an end to these depraved cities.

On the opposite end of the spectrum however, believers in Christ can look forward to an ideal place to live. Hebrews 11:16 (ESV) says, "But as it is, they desire a better country, that is, a heavenly one. Therefore God is not ashamed to be called their God, for He has prepared for them a city." We know that this city will be free of all forms of sin, including crime and depravity. The foundations of the city will be made from all sorts of jewels and gold (Revelation 21:19-21). "But nothing unclean will ever enter it, nor anyone who does what is detestable or false, but only those who are written in the Lamb's book of life," declares Revelation 21:27 (ESV). How do you get your name in that book and get to see the Great City? Just have faith in the ultimate Hero – Jesus Christ!

BATMAN RETURNS

In 1992, Warner Brothers released *Batman Returns*, the follow-up to Tim Burton's first foray into the world of the Dark Knight. Despite its enormous box-office earnings, the film was polarizing to both fans and critics. A darker and more bizarre film than its predecessor, *Batman Returns* finds Bruce Wayne navigating threats in his both public life and his secret one. Bruce is having to aid Gotham's mayor against Max Schreck, another wealthy businessman and industrialist looking to build a huge power plant and monopolize the city's power grid. As Batman, he is also having to contend with a circus-themed gang that is working for a new criminal known as the Penguin. Finally, there's Selina Kyle who creates her own alter ego in Catwoman, whose motivations are fuzzy at best.

If there is one cohesive theme present in this movie, it's lust. Each of the characters here can be seen lusting for something. The film's two antagonists, Penguin and Max Schreck, both lust for power and prestige. Their mutual desires make them natural allies. Penguin is a freak of nature, a man with animal-like characteristics whose origin is explained in the film's prologue. His parents abandoned him in the sewers when they saw his bird-like appearance. Having lived underneath Gotham for thirty years, Penguin kidnaps Schreck and enlists his help to usher him into society. Schreck agrees as long as Penguin returns the favor in helping take down Gotham's mayor. Eventually, the plan blows up in their faces and they both turn on one another.

Selina Kyle also succumbs to lust in this film; her desire for physical and emotional gratification corrupt her. Her origin here strays quite a bit from the comics. This version of Selina is a put upon and quiet secretary for Schreck. High strung and nervous, she is lacking confidence in numerous ways. Late one night trying to catch up on work, she discovers documents relating to Schreck's planned monopoly. Refusing to risk her ruining his plans, Schreck knocks her out the window. Seemingly falling to her death, Selina is instead knocked unconscious in a nearby alley. She is awakened when numerous cats lick and nibble on her. Suddenly, Selina is almost an entirely different person. She gives into a repressed impulsive nature, designs a costume, and becomes Catwoman. Her attraction to Batman and desire for vengeance on Schreck is her attempt to validate her self-worth.

Lastly, even Batman himself is not above being tempted by lust in this film. He meets Selina both in and out of costume. Each way, he senses something of a kindred spirit, particularly because of the dual lives they both lead. Of course, there is no nobility in Selina's double life as compared to Bruce's and soon the lines are blurred for Batman. Catwoman serves as a distraction for Batman while Penguin campaigns for mayor and poisons Gotham's political climate. At the climax of the film, Batman tries to convince Catwoman that they both can give up their costumes and live happily together. Tragically, she chooses vengeance on Shreck instead.

Lust is a sin that the Bible spends many pages rebuking. Famously, one of the Ten Commandments is not to commit adultery (Exodus 20:14). It is not enough to avoid engaging in adulterous acts either. "But I say to you that everyone who looks at a woman with lustful intent has already committed adultery with her in his heart," Jesus says in Matthew 5:28 (ESV). We cannot allow even our thoughts towards someone to be lustful, such as Bruce's and Selina's towards each other. Our bodies are not meant for sexual immorality but for serving the Lord (1 Corinthians 6:13).

There are other things that we can lust for though, such as power and recognition. These are the things that we all want at times, as did Schreck,

Penguin, and Selina as well. None were content in their lives, they wanted more. We need to learn to be content with what we have (Hebrews 13:5) and not lust after things or esteem. The world is full of such things to pull us away and tempt us into evil doings, things like what Max Schreck did. "For everything in the world – the lust of the flesh, the lust of the eyes, and the pride of life – comes not from the Father but from the world," says 1 John 2:16 (NIV). When you desire the things of the world, you become part of the world and act like it.

It's easy even for the noblest to be done in by the allure of things the world offers. Remember Paul's advice in 2 Timothy 2:22 (ESV). "So flee youthful passions and pursue righteousness, faith, love, and peace, along with those who call on the Lord from a pure heart."

Two-Face

*B*atman: The Animated Series was developed by Warner Brothers after the success of the two live-action films. Debuting in 1992, it is considered by many to be the pinnacle of depictions of Batman.

Two of the most acclaimed episodes of the animated series ever produced are "Two-Face," parts one and two. Differing in some ways from the origin and portrayal seen in the comics and other media, the animated series presents him as a particularly tragic figure. One of the changes is that Harvey Dent is not simply an ally of Batman, but actually a close friend of Bruce Wayne. The two have known each other for years and Bruce has been a supporter of Dent's reelection campaign. This makes their hero and villain rivalry all the more personal. Another added element is Harvey's extreme temper and a second personality that he has been hiding since a young boy. It flares up in public on two different occasions, forcing Harvey to seek professional help.

Eventually, Rupert Thorne, one of Gotham's biggest mobsters and Dent's current target, obtains the dirt on Harvey and blackmails him with it. There is a confrontation between Dent and Thorne's gang at a chemical plant. In an explosion, Dent is scarred and subsequently becomes Two-Face. He then goes on a mission to humiliate Thorne by destroying all of his businesses and then plans to end him once and for all. Meanwhile,

Thorne uses Dent's fiancé Grace as a ploy to draw Two-Face out. Grace hasn't seen him in six months and she unwittingly leads Thorne right to him.

The scene between Two-Face and Grace is a bittersweet one. Holed up inside of an old ballroom, the room is a manifestation of Two-Face's personality. Half the room is cast in shadow, the other in light. Grace asks what's happened to him and why he longer listens to his feelings, the way he used to. "This is what I listen to now," Two-Face says, flipping his coin in the air. "Chance, Grace. Chance is everything. Whether you're born or not, whether you live or die, whether you're good or bad; it's all arbitrary!" Grace rejects this and asks him if it was chance that made them fall in love or made him a brilliant district attorney. She pleads with him to take control of his life.

Many people look at their lives and feel like they are victims of their circumstances. They may blame others for the choices they've made. They may even blame God Himself and question Him for the mistakes they've made. Some people may believe, like Two-Face, that everything is just luck of the draw. There is no reason for anything and it's all arbitrary. But anyone who has a strong faith in the Lord knows this isn't true. We know that God has a plan and every detail planned out. Paul wrote in Ephesians 2:10 (ESV), "For we are his workmanship, created in Christ Jesus for good works, which God prepared beforehand, that we should walk in them." Jesus said that that a sparrow can't fall to the ground without the Father knowing (Matthew 10:29). If God knows the number of hairs on our head (Luke 12:7), then we can know that our lives are not just made up of random events.

Yet, we must also take responsibility for our mistakes and the natural consequences that follow. We never get away with the results of our sins, although God is always willing to forgive. David was a great man of God but he made the terrible mistake of adultery and then murder. God forgave him but also said that David would have to suffer the costs of his sins (2 Samuel 12:13-14). When we put God behind us and forget Him, we will come off the path He has for us and fall in the face of temptation. That has nothing to do with random chance but our own foolishness.

We can't be like Two-Face and allow the troubles we face in life to cause us to doubt God's plan or His love for us. Always keep in mind how much God loves you. We know He has every step of our lives planned out. Remind yourself daily with the classic verse in Jeremiah 29:11. "For I know the plans I have for you, declares the Lord, plans for welfare and not for evil, to give you a future and a hope."

MR. FREEZE

Mr. Freeze was once considered one of the campiest villains in Batman's infamous rogue's gallery. Debuting in 1959 as Mr. Zero, Freeze became popularized by his portrayal in the 1960s TV series. Mr. Freeze was not much beyond a gimmick; he committed cold-related crimes. The character was so shallow that DC even killed him off in *Robin II: The Joker's Wild #1*. However, in the seminal *Batman: The Animated Series*, writer Paul Dini would revive the character with a new, tragic take on the villain.

"Heart of Ice" tells the story of Victor Fries (pronounced Freeze), a scientist specializing in cryogenics, whose wife is terminally ill. Utilizing tools at his employer's company GothCorp, Fries is secretly conducting an experiment that will hopefully keep his wife Nora alive long enough to find a cure. However, GothCorp CEO Ferris Boyle interrupts the experiment with security guards in tow and during the ensuing fight, there's an explosion. Cryogenic chemicals spray everywhere, interacting with the equipment, leaving Victor Fries permanently genetically altered. From that moment on, he needs a specialized suit to survive above subzero temperatures. It also leaves him bloodthirsty for revenge on the man who ruined both his life and his chance to save his wife.

The newly christened Mr. Freeze begins hunting down Ferris Boyle and Batman must stop Freeze before he harms anyone who might get in the way. The episode climaxes at a gala where Boyle is set to receive a Humanitarian of the Year award (ironically contrasting his public image with his secret cruelty toward Fries). Vengeance is nearly within Mr. Freeze's grasp before Batman is able to finally bring him down. However, the lynch pin of the episode is Batman's empathy for Freeze and his quest for true justice to be served. Batman hands over video evidence of the accident and tells of how Boyle is responsible for destroying two innocent lives.

The Bible often warns of seeking vengeance for personal wrongs. Jesus said in Matthew 5:38 (ESV), "You have heard that it was said, 'An eye for an eye and a tooth for a tooth.' But I say to you, do not resist the one who is evil. But if anyone slaps you on the right cheek, turn to him the other also." Even in the harshest of wrongs, such as what happened to Victor Fries, we must not succumb to our desires for vengeance. Paul wrote in Romans 12:19 (ESV), "Beloved, never avenge yourselves, but leave it to the wrath of God, for it is written, 'Vengeance is mine, I will repay, says the Lord.'" We must always pray for the strength to allow God to right the wrongs in our lives for us. Pray for the people who hurt you and ask God to give you the strength to do so. Then one day, just as Batman delivered justice for Fries and his wife Nora, God will do so for all of us.

"He will bring forth your righteousness as the light, and your justice as the noonday," Psalms 37:6 (ESV).

POISON IVY

There are many foes in Batman's rogues gallery but one of the most dangerous of all might be Pamela Isley aka Poison Ivy. A former Gotham City botanist who turns to crime, Ivy has contempt for humanity and loves only things that grow from the ground. Plants are her priority, not people. Poison Ivy often carries potions, poisons, and other chemical combinations in her arsenal. However, her deadliest weapon is one the Bible warns about constantly – sexual temptation.

Poison Ivy can seduce nearly anyone with the use of her plant pheromones to accomplish her goals. Once her toxins are in you, it's nearly impossible to snap out of the trance. She is sometimes depicted almost like a siren, who slowly lures in her victims through seduction. Ivy does exactly this to Bruce Wayne in *Batman: The Long Halloween*. Bruce is first infected with one of her contaminants and slowly, he succumbs to her mind-control. Lucky for him, Catwoman comes to his aid.

In the *Batman: The Animated Series* episode "Pretty Poison" Pamela Isley is first introduced as a woman dating Harvey Dent. While at dinner together, Isley gives Dent a passionate kiss goodbye. Little does Dent know her lipstick is laced with a toxin and he literally passes out into his dessert. Batman tracks her down and eventually is able to procure the antidote.

Sexual temptation might be the toughest challenge we face in this world. It is insidious and often the toughest sin to resist. But we must because it directly affects our bodies. "Flee from sexual immorality. Every other sin a person commits is outside the body, but the sexually immoral person sins against his own body," Paul writes in 1 Corinthians 6:18 (ESV). The Holy Spirit dwells in our bodies. We are temples for Him and while any sin grieves Him, sexual sins are the worst of all. God designed sex and our attraction to the opposite sex for marriage; nothing else (Genesis 2:24). 1 Corinthians 7:2 (ESV) says, "But because of the temptation to sexual immorality, each man should have his own wife and each woman her own husband."

We must be on guard for when the Enemy tries to tempt us in this vulnerable area. Always be aware of a way out if necessary. God will always give us a means of escape. "No temptation has overtaken you that is not common to man. God is faithful, and he will not let you be tempted beyond your ability, but with the temptation he will also provide the way of escape, that you may be able to endure it," Paul says in 1 Corinthians 10:13 (ESV). Even if you have to literally run away just like Joseph did from Potiphar's wife (Genesis 39) it is surely worth it to avoid sinning in such a terrible way.

Even someone as great as David fell into this very trap when he slept with Bathsheba. Not only did he sleep with another man's wife but he then killed that man in order to cover it up (2 Samuel 11)! One terrible sin can often lead to another. It is like this when Poison Ivy has her victims in her clutches. First, they're tempted sexually and then they're doing her bidding for other crimes. Avoid sexual temptation at all costs. It's poison!

"His Silicon Soul"

When three criminals break into an abandoned warehouse belonging to a once-thriving robotics company, the last thing they expect to find is Batman hidden inside a large crate. Horrified, they run for their lives but are quickly pursued by him. One of them opens fire at Batman but the bullets do nothing. The thug runs screaming, "You're not human!" Batman looks down, perplexed. There are chords, cables, and machinery hanging out from his now torn costume.

Such is the opening for the *Batman: The Animated Series* episode "His Silicon Soul" written by Marty Isenberg and Robert N. Skir. The episode follows up on a previous story that revolved around an evil artificial intelligence named HARDAC, who tried to replace humankind with robotic duplicates. Batman was able to shut the program down and HARDAC's factory was dismantled. Unbeknownst to the authorities, HARDAC created one last duplicate – a copy of Batman and it had been sitting in this warehouse ever since. Once awoken by the burglars, the Batman duplicate begins investigating, believing himself to really be Batman.

The duplicate and the real Batman first encounter one another at the house of Karl Rossum, the scientist responsible for originally creating HARDAC. A fight ensues between Batman and his robotic doppelganger in Rossum's greenhouse. Damage occurs to the structure and Rossum is at risk of being crushed by debris. The robot sees Rossum in danger and knocks him out of the way as the ceiling caves in. Batman searches for the robot but it is nowhere to be found.

The robot in fact survived the collapse and discovers a software chip that sheds light on his origin. Coming to grips that he is just a robotic clone, he inserts the chip into his metal body and his operating system is reset. HARDAC now exists in the robot's mind and the mission to replace humanity begins again.

This all comes to a head as Batman tracks the duplicate back to the batcave. The duplicate is in the process of uploading HARDAC to the cave's mainframe computer. The screen is counting down from five minutes before HARDAC is alive and spread all over the world. As the two of them fight each other, Batman insists the duplicate is too good a copy of himself; that it can't kill, as evidenced by it going out of its way to save Rossum in the greenhouse earlier. The duplicate continues to fight Batman however and corners him to a cliff. The duplicate takes a swing at Batman, knocking him over. The robot tries to grab him but Batman falls into darkness, seemingly to his death. The robot is horrified and laments that he's taken a life. With mere seconds left on the upload, he screams, "My city! My people! What have I done?" He destroys the computer and it explodes, destroying the robot duplicate in the process. Batman, of course, is alive and inspects the duplicate with Alfred. He comments, "Could it be it had a soul, Alfred? A soul of silicon, but a soul nonetheless?"

To answer Bruce's question, no, it could not have a soul. Mankind can only create pale imitations of what the Creator God can imbue with His life. We know God created the world and then put man in it (Genesis 1:27). Everything good comes from God but the most valuable is the soul. Jesus asked, "For what will it profit a man if he gains the whole world and forfeits his soul? Or what shall a man give in return for his soul?" We know that man and woman can create life but that too is a gift from God. We can't create something like the soul on our own, nor can we imbue anything we make with a soul. Artificial intelligence like HARDAC can't be achieved in the real world and without the souls God gave us, it would be cold and lifeless. When the duplicate is fighting Batman, it says HARDAC's new world will be free of crime, suffering, or frailty. Batman responds it would also be free of compassion and free of choice. The latter two are more gifts from God. A world free of crime, suffering, and frailty will eventually be established by Jesus (Revelation 22). This will be achieved through God, not man-made means. Anything made by us just lacks His touch.

"For you formed my inward parts; you knitted me together in my mother's womb. I praise you, for I am fearfully and wonderfully made. Wonderful are your works; my soul knows it very well," Psalms 139: 13-14 (ESV).

SCARECROW

Fear is an emotion we have all experienced at some point in our lives and this is especially true for the denizens of Gotham City. Crime is often at an all-time high and the police are often powerless to help. One villain in particular thrives on spreading fear everywhere he goes. That would be Johnathan Crane, aka the Scarecrow. Crane was obsessed with fear as a child and this obsession only continued into adulthood. He eventually earned a Ph.D. in Psychology and became a professor at Gotham University. Soon though, the university fired Crane for his illegal experimentation on both people and animals. Humiliated, he took on an alter ego, the Scarecrow, and began spreading his fear toxin all over Gotham.

The Bible often tells us not to worry or be afraid. Deuteronomy 31:8 (ESV) says, "It is the Lord who goes before you. He will be with you; He will not leave you or forsake you. Do not fear or be dismayed." God wants us to fear nothing and always rely on His strength to face our fears. Paul reminds us in Philippians 4:6-7 (ESV) "Do not be anxious about anything, but in everything by prayer and supplication with thanksgiving let your requests be made known to God. And the peace of God, which surpasses all understanding, will guard your hearts and minds in Christ Jesus."

We all have fears in our life that we must overcome. Sometimes it is a phobia, sometimes an outcome in our relationships or jobs, and other times it is simply the world's troubles, such as wars and diseases. When these things come over us as strong as Scarecrow's fear toxin, there's only one cure – the supernatural peace of knowing God. Take David's advice from Psalm 56:3 (ESV). "When I am afraid, I put my trust in You." God is sovereign. He controls everything. Jesus said that a sparrow cannot hit the ground without God knowing (Matthew 10:29). He knows the fears that we are facing and He is more than willing to give us the strength and courage that we need.

There is only one kind of fear that the Bible endorses and that's the fear of the Lord. Psalms 25:14 (ESV) says, "The friendship of the Lord is for those who fear Him, and He makes known to them His covenant." Also in Psalms 33:8 (ESV), "Let all the earth fear the Lord; let all the inhabitants of the world stand in awe of Him!" This is a different kind of fear; one of respect. It is like how a child needs to fear and respect his or her parents. It does not mean we are afraid of God, because perfect love drives out fear (1 John 4:18). God deserves our fear and respect for who He is and what He does for us each and every day. Such is the only kind of fear that is good for us.

Satan spreads fear as well just like the Scarecrow. If you are a follower of Christ, the Enemy will attack and paralyze you with fear so that you cannot do the Lord's work. Like Scarecrow's fear toxin, Satan's fear can poison our mind, heart, and spirit. When there's any kind of opening in our spiritual armor, one little seed of doubt is all it takes to turn into a mountain of worry and stress. Satan starts with a whisper and his fear then can spread like a virus. When that happens we must turn to God in trust and His peace will calm us.

So when the Enemy tries to scare us or intimidate us, inscribe Psalms 56:11 (ESV) on your heart. "In God I trust; I shall not be afraid. What can man do to me?"

HARLEY QUINN

Harley Quinn is one of the most recent additions to Batman's canon and yet she has proven to be wildly successful, arguably the single most popular character from the animated series. She debuted in the episode "Joker's Favor" which aired on September 11, 1992. Harley Quinn (voiced by Arleen Sorkin) was created by writer Paul Dini with the intention of simply being the Joker's henchwoman. She was a tribute to the female gangster girls of the 1940s. In her red and black harlequin costume and with her high-pitched Brooklyn accent, Harley immediately became a fan-favorite.

However, it was later that Harley was finally given the depth the character deserved. "Mad Love" was published as a standalone comic by Bruce Timm and Paul Dini in 1994. The story was eventually adapted into a series episode, which aired on January 16, 1999. It explored who Harley was and where she came from before she became the Joker's sidekick. Her real name is Harleen Quinzel and she has a PhD in Psychology. Harleen has just earned an internship at Arkham Asylum and even before she has laid eyes on the Joker, she has a fascination with psychotic personalities. She comments to her supervisor on the "glamor" of these extreme characters. When they've finished their tour, Harley hears an intoxicating whistling coming from down the hallway. Here, she first meets the Joker at the door of his cell, who seductively winks at her. Harleen is fascinated and she arranges for Joker to be her first patient. He remarks that her name reminds him of a harlequin and Harleen says that she's heard that one before. Their sessions continue and Joker wins over her sympathy with tales of an abusive, alcoholic father. Harleen characterizes the Joker as misunderstood and traumatized by his childhood and blames Batman for the Joker's bad reputation. The breaking point for Harleen comes when Joker escapes and goes on another crime spree. Batman returns the Joker to Arkham battered and bruised. Harleen snaps, dons a costume, and breaks Joker out of the asylum, declaring herself his "new and improved Harley Quinn." The rest of Mad Love takes place in the present day, with Harley capturing Batman in an attempt to prove herself to the Joker. However, Batman tells Harley that all of Joker's stories of his abusive childhood were manipulative lies. He simply wanted to corrupt his newest psychiatrist.

What happened to Harley Quinn is a tragic tale and we all are susceptible to the same tragedy every day. There is someone worse than the Joker out there in the world who would like nothing more than to tempt and destroy us as well. The Bible says, "Your adversary the devil prowls around like a roaring lion, seeking someone to devour" (1 Peter 5:8 ESV). The devil often tries to tempt us with what we want. Harleen Quinzel's attraction to the Joker first stemmed from her greed and desire for fame. She arrived at Arkham looking to write books on the glamorous criminals of Gotham. Joker offered to share his "secrets" with her. From there, he gained her sympathies and caused her to turn. This is exactly how Satan works. "But each person is tempted when he is lured and enticed by his own desire," the Bible says in James 1:14 (ESV). Satan baits us with something we think we need and reels us in. The next thing we know, we are deep in sinful behavior. Harley went from a promising psychiatrist to a costumed criminal seeking love from someone who doesn't understand love. Batman says to her, "The Joker doesn't love anyone but himself." But Harley blames Batman for all her troubles and refuses to take responsibility for her own mistakes. We can treat God the same way. He only tries to help us and lead us away from forces that might destroy us, but we oftentimes blame God because of choices we have made. James wrote in 1:13 of his letter, "Let no one say when he is tempted, 'I am being tempted by God,' for God cannot be tempted with evil, and He Himself tempts no one.'" God doesn't put these stumbling blocks in our paths, it is our Enemy. God only wants us to overcome these things.

At the end of "Mad Love" Harley decides that she's finally had enough of the Joker and his abuse. But ultimately, he manipulates her again and again and Harley returns to him again and again. Don't allow yourself to fall into the trap of temptation and sin. Once Jesus rescues you from sin, don't allow yourself to go back, like Harley Quinn.

"Like a dog that returns to his vomit is a fool who repeats his folly," Proverbs 26:11 ESV

BARBARA GORDON

In 1998, *Batman & Mr. Freeze: Subzero* was released directly to video to much critical acclaim. Spinning off from the animated series, *Subzero* follows Mr. Freeze, who is now living in the Arctic alongside an adopted Eskimo boy named Koonak, two polar bears, and his wife Nora, who is still cryogenically asleep. It is an idyllic lifestyle for Freeze, who is able to live freely without the use of his suit in such frigid temperatures. Unfortunately, Freeze's paradise is shattered when a research submarine unknowingly comes to the surface under their home. The hull destroys the ice and in the process, Nora's cryogenic chamber is ruptured. With the chamber no longer functioning, her body will continue to deteriorate from her illness. Freeze is horrified, and after taking revenge upon the submarine's crew, returns to Gotham to seek help for his wife.

Mr. Freeze confronts a former colleague, Dr. Gregory Belson, demanding his help to cure his dying wife. It is decided that Nora needs an organ donor and she is of a rare blood type. When Belson fails to find any available donors, Freeze insists they use a live donor. At first Belson refuses, but is convinced when Freeze tempts him with gold from the arctic. Belson is in dire financial troubles and the allure of money seduces him. The perfect donor turns out to be none other than Barbara Gordon, whom they kidnap and bring to an offshore oil rig near Gotham.

Batman and Robin eventually track Barbara to the oil rig and find her being chased by Freeze and Belson. A stray bullet fired by Belson nicks a fuel tank and causes an explosion. Soon, the entire rig is engulfed in flame and Freeze becomes pinned by falling debris. He implores Belson to help him get Nora to safety but Belson betrays him and subsequently dies in an attempt to flee.

Barbara sees Freeze trapped and tries to help him. In spite of everything Freeze had done to her, Barbara stayed true to her character and did the right thing. She calls to Batman and Robin for help and together, they fight through the flames and retrieve Nora. On the way out, Freeze seemingly plummets to his death while the rest of the group escapes in the Batwing. While the world assumes Freeze is dead, he actually makes it back to the Arctic and discovers that Nora is alive. The Wayne Foundation funded an organ transplant to save her life and Freeze is moved to tears.

Compassion for one's enemies is something the Bible stresses to us. Jesus said, "Love your enemies and pray for those who persecute you" (Matthew 5:44). Jesus also famously forgave his persecutors when He was on the cross (Luke 23:34). Others in the Bible have forgiven their enemies as they've been threatened or even killed. In Acts 7:60, Stephen asks God not to hold the sin of his death against his killers.

Barbara could have left Freeze to die on the oil rig. After all, he did kidnap her and was going to kill her in order to save his wife. But Barbara took pity on him and tried to save him anyway. Likewise, Batman did what he could to rescue Nora and was visibly devastated when Freeze fell into the ocean. On the other hand, Belson did not even think twice about leaving Mr. Freeze behind if it meant saving his own life. He was willing to kill someone he didn't even know simply for money.

In our everyday lives when we're wronged, instead of reacting in an angry way, even if that anger is justified, we should react the way Barbara Gordon did. Respond with forgiveness, prayer, and a willingness to help.

Batman: The Animated Series

"I am the Night"

"I am the Night" is written by Michael Reaves and is an episode that truly explores Batman as both man and hero. It opens with Alfred finding Batman sitting in the cave (in a chair carved out of the rock wall no less) absolutely exhausted. He is pondering the seeming futility of his mission and his life. When Alfred reminds Batman of the lives he's saved and the criminals he's caught, he dismisses them as "a few fires put out." Batman remarks about how the war goes on and on and then asks Alfred if he has the package. He has an appointment to keep.

It is the anniversary of his parents' death and every year, Batman ventures out to Crime Alley, the area where the Waynes were killed. In the package are two red roses that Batman lays down in honor of his parents. He typically meets Leslie Thompkins, a psychotherapist who took care of Bruce as a child. She is one of few who know his secret identity. While there, Batman overhears a scuffle from down the street. A young grifter nicknamed Wizard is being roughed up by two mobsters. Batman makes quick work of them and asks Leslie to take Wizard to the shelter where she works.

In the meantime, Commissioner Gordon is preparing a raid on a gang led by a mobster called the Jazzman. He's been waiting on Batman, who has been delayed by the scuffle in the alley. Gordon can't wait any longer

29

and sends his men inside. Batman does eventually arrive and chases down the Jazzman, who is escaping in a large truck. Batman derails him but is horrified to see that Gordon was hurt in the process.

Batman hasn't eaten or slept in days, having resigned himself to the cave. Dick Grayson goes to talk some sense into him.

"I should have been there sooner!" Batman insists.

"You can't be everywhere! You're only human! You do all one man can, more than one man is expected to do!" Dick argues.

Batman won't hear it though and vows that no one else will get hurt because of his mistakes. He rips his mask off and tosses it into the abyss inside the cave. Batman is finished.

Of course, it isn't long before trouble brews again. The Jazzman escapes Gotham Penitentiary and his next move is to finish off Jim Gordon, who is in the hospital. Dick tries to shake a despondent Bruce Wayne into action, saying, "You taught me everything I know about crime fighting, Bruce, but the most important lesson was to never give up!"

Finally, Batman takes action and goes to Gotham General just in time to stop the Jazzman from killing Jim Gordon.

The two allies spend a few moments together before Batman departs to patrol the city once more. He spies the grifter, Wizard, waiting outside a bus terminal. Batman confronts him, assuming Wizard has stolen the briefcase he's holding. But, in fact, Wizard is the owner and tells Batman that the experience at the shelter gave him a change of heart. He's heading home to his folks and leaving his life of crime behind him. After a sincere thank you, Wizard boards his bus leaving Batman surprised but pleased. He returns to the rooftops, overlooks his city, and leaves us with the rarest of images; Batman with a smile on his face.

We have all been where Batman is at the start of this episode. The cares of the world, the struggle to remain on the path God has laid for us; simply the efforts to do good in the world can be crushing. The Enemy does his best to trip us up and cause us to tire. It is truly exhausting not only physically but emotionally and spiritually. Batman remarks, "A weary body can be dealt with, but a weary spirit? That's something else."

God knows this is the case as well. He created rest for a reason (Genesis 2:1-3). "Come to me, all who labor and are heavy laden, and I will give you rest. Take my yoke upon you, and learn from me, for I am gentle and lowly in heart, and you will find rest for your souls," Jesus says in Matthew 11:28-29 (ESV). When we reach this point of exhaustion, Jesus can renew us. He can restore our bodies and our souls.

The lesson here is not just simply about exhaustion, though. We may also find ourselves in situations where our best efforts, the efforts to bring a friend or family member to Jesus, to get a degree, to raise our kids, or just to do good simply have no results. We can be like Batman where we question our reasons or motivation to move ahead when there seems to be no end in sight. Paul wrote in 2 Thessalonians 3:13 (ESV), "As for you, brothers, do not grow weary in doing good." Also in Galatians 6:9 (ESV) Paul wrote, "And let us not grow weary of doing good, for in due season we will reap, if we do not give up." This is what Dick said Bruce taught him earlier in life, to never give up. We must keep going even when we feel our work will not pay off. It will, just as it did for Batman when he not only saved Gordon's life, but when he discovered the positive impact he had on Wizard.

We don't have to be superheroes to do good though. We can simply pray to our Heavenly Father and He will supply us with what we need. We are still only human and we need His power to do great things. It's like Dick told Batman, he can't be everywhere and neither can we. Only the Holy Spirit can do that and we need Him to accomplish what we're called to do. So take Paul's advice in 1 Thessalonians 5:17 and "pray without ceasing." It will pay off in the end.

Batman: The Animated Series

"It's Never Too Late"

O ne of the greatest episodes of the animated series is "It's Never Too Late" a harrowing crime thriller by Tom Reugger with the teleplay by Garin Wolf. It revolves around an aging mob boss named Arnold Stromwell who is struggling to keep his criminal empire together while searching for his missing son Joey. Stromwell arranges for a meeting with his chief rival, Rupert Thorne, with the intention of a truce and also to get a lead on his son's whereabouts. Thorne agrees to the meeting but in fact has a double cross planned. Thorne has planted a bomb inside the restaurant where they meet.

Meanwhile, Batman learns of the meeting and goes to visit Stromwell's brother Michael, who is a priest at a Gotham cathedral. At first he is startled to see Batman in his doorway asking for help. "It's coming down tonight, Father. He's going to need you."

Father Michael shakes his head. "Arnold? That's one soul I wish I could give up on," he sighs.

"I don't believe you'd give up on anyone, Father. Please be there," Batman encourages him.

Batman then gets to the meeting between Stromwell and Thorne just in time to save Stromwell from the blast. He then takes Stromwell to the Sunrise Foundation, a drug addiction rehab center. Stromwell is shocked to find his son there, laying in agony in a hospital bed. His ex-wife Connie is already in the room and Stromwell demands to know why she didn't call him. She replies that she only found out that day, thanks to Batman. Stromwell becomes angry, promising that he'll find the guy that got Joey hooked. But Connie tells Arnold that it was him and his people who push drugs that ruined Joey's life. She remarks that she left him to get away from all of that but Joey wasn't as lucky. Batman beseeches Stromwell to help put an end to it. "All your power and money have bought you is an empire of misery!" Batman tells him.

Arnold agrees to talk to the district attorney and so they head to his office to get all of his records. But when they arrive and Batman is looking over the records, he realizes they're fakes. Stromwell has double-crossed him and holds Batman at gunpoint. On top of that, Rupert Thorne and his men show up as well and begin attacking.

During the fight, Stromwell is flushed out into a nearby train yard. Flashbacks to his youth come upon of him. He sees his younger self and his brother Michael walking along the railroad tracks. Young Arnold is bragging about how when he grows up, he's going to own the city. While arguing with one another, they realize that a train is coming. Arnold is paralyzed with fear and can't get out of the way. Michael acts quickly and shoves his brother out of the way, which we discover has cost him his leg later in life. He now has a prosthetic.

Arnold asks Michael why he saved him all those years ago. "You knew I was no good," Stromwell laments.

"Arnie, what else could I do? But now you have a chance to save yourself. Come on, Arnie, do the right thing; for yourself, for your son, for me, your little brother!"

Thorne comes on them suddenly with a gun, mocking their "little family reunion." Batman quickly appears and dispatches Thorne just as the police arrive. Commissioner Gordon approaches and Stromwell says he has a statement to give him. Batman watches from above and then turns and looks down the street. Off in the distance, glowing like a light in the darkness, is Father Michael's church.

We may have people in our lives just like the young Arnie Stromwell. They have big plans for their lives, big ambitions, and those plans may not always be good. In fact, they may be completely misguided plans. Such people need to focus their eyes on God so that they won't be led astray by the devil's lies. Proverbs 3:6 (ESV) says, "In all your ways acknowledge Him, and He will make straight your paths." We need the people in our lives to encourage us to remain true to our faith and to God. Just like Michael did for his brother Arnold, we have to be there for our friends and family when they need us. Oftentimes that may be extremely difficult for us. Relationships may be strained or we might think that a particular loved one is beyond all hope. Just like Michael laments to Batman that he wishes he could give up on Arnie, we might want to stop trying to help. But we must not lose hope because God can reach anyone.

Another section of scripture reflected in the episode is James 1:11. "For the sun rises with its scorching heat and withers the grass; its flower falls, and its beauty perishes. So also will the rich man fade away in the midst of his pursuits." James writes again in 5:1, "Come now, you rich, weep and howl for the miseries that are coming upon you." Batman points out to Stromwell how miserable his life has become in spite of his money and power. His marriage is shattered, his empire is crumbling, and his son is clinging to life because of Stromwell's drug pushers. His riches meant nothing at that point.

Finally, there is the scene between the now fully grown Michael and Arnold, standing on the same kind of railroad tracks where Michael lost his leg to save his brother. Everything is coming to a head for Stromwell. He is overcome with the guilt of his brother's injury, not to mention his son's condition and what he's done to Gotham. His question to Michael, about why Michael saved a person who is no good, is an honest one. Arnold's answer is also honest. What other response is there when you love someone? It's the same response we get when we ask God why He saved us. He loves in spite of our failings and our sin. Romans 5:8 (ESV) says, "But God shows His love for us in that while we were still sinners,

Christ died for us." We weren't any good either before Jesus sacrificed His life for us. But out of love, He gave us a chance.

So when you feel worthless or lost or when you need help with someone you love who is lost, do what Batman does at the end of this episode. Look to the Church and the Power behind it.

Batman: Mask of the Phantasm

ANDREA BEAUMONT

O n Christmas 1993, Warner Brothers released the animated feature
film *Batman: Mask of the Phantasm*, which delves into territory
not explored in *Batman: The Animated Series*. Examining Bruce Wayne's
days before donning the cape and cowl, the movie is a tragic love story
between him and a woman named Andrea Beaumont.

At this stage of his life, Bruce has been back in Gotham for a short
while and is just exploring putting his mission into action. However,
the sudden introduction of Andrea has cast his undertaking into doubt.
They fall in love and it quickly becomes apparent to Bruce that he cannot risk his life while someone is waiting for him at home. Instead, he
proposes to Andrea but Bruce is shocked when the ring is returned back
to him the following day via messenger. There is a letter attached from
Andrea turning down his proposal, saying she's leaving for Europe with
her father. Stunned and heartbroken, Bruce returns to his intention of
ridding Gotham City of crime.

Ten years later, the biggest mobsters in Gotham are being hunted down
by a mysterious ghostly figure called the Phantasm. Few have seen this
new vigilante up close and many, including Gotham's new district attorney, actually suspect Batman is behind the mobsters' deaths. Meanwhile,
Andrea Beaumont returns to Gotham to tend to her father's estate. Bruce

and Andrea encounter one another and Bruce contemplates resuming their relationship. However this thought is premature as he begins to put the pieces together. Andrea's father, Carl, is the connection between these mobsters. He had owed them a great deal of money and fled to Europe with Andrea ten years earlier, which is why she had turned down Bruce's proposal. At first Bruce suspects that her father is the Phantasm but soon realizes Andrea is actually the new vigilante.

In spite of paying his debts to the mob, Carl Beaumont was killed by their hit man, the one who would eventually become the Joker. He is the last of Andrea's targets and she meets him at his hideout, an abandoned world's fair. Batman eventually catches up to her and begs her to give up her crusade. Andrea refuses, explaining to Bruce how the mob took everything from her; her father, her friends, her relationship with him, and her life. She insists that they had to pay.

Batman asks, "But Andie, what will vengeance solve?"

Andrea coldly responds, "If anyone knows the answer to that, Bruce, it's you."

Dumbfounded, he implores her to leave and Andrea finally relents. Batman proceeds to chase down the Joker, who has planted several time bombs underneath the grounds. Eventually, Batman catches Joker but not before the explosions go off. Andrea reappears and takes the Joker with her and Batman is forced to escape the blast.

The film ends with Alfred consoling Bruce in the batcave. He's devastated that he wasn't able to save Andrea. Alfred responds that Andrea didn't want to be saved. He continues, "Vengeance blackens the soul, Bruce. I've always feared that you would become that which you fought against. You walk the edge of that abyss every night but you haven't and I thank Heaven for that. But Andrea fell into that pit years ago and no one, not even you could have held her back."

The last we see of Andrea is on a cruise ship at an unknown location, presumably miles from Gotham. When a man is trying to flirt with her and asks if she'd rather be alone, she dejectedly responds, "I am."

Andrea Beaumont suffered some of the worst and most tragic losses

an individual can face. It is understandable that she would thirst for justice. But she allowed that thirst to fester and spin out of control. Perhaps
one of the most difficult things that the Bible asks us to do is let God
avenge us. We cannot go after those who hurt us. It only does more harm
than good. 1 Peter 3:9 (NIV) says, "Do not repay evil with evil or insult
with insult. On the contrary, repay evil with blessing, because to this you
were called so that you may inherit a blessing."

It's true that Batman straddles that line but Andrea concocted her
plans purely to satisfy her own needs and killed in order to get it. Such is
a line that Batman did not cross and his ultimate goal was to help other
people. Of course in the real world, we must not take things into our own
hands at all and have to wait on God. Proverbs 20:22 (ESV) says, "Do not
say, 'I will repay evil'; wait for the Lord, and He will deliver you."

Jesus also tells us while praying to forgive others so that the Father
can forgive us as well (Mark 11:25). It isn't a natural response but a supernatural response. If not handed over to the Lord, the thirst for revenge
will blacken your soul just as it did to Andrea. It will render you isolated
and alone like her. That is ultimately the Enemy's goal – to isolate believers from each other. If we are not with other believers, then we cannot
receive the love and encouragement we need in our lives. Then our relationship with God will suffer too. Resist the temptation of revenge and let
God repay wrongdoings!

ROBIN

atman has always been a lasting and popular character. Many things spring to mind in association with him but perhaps the first and foremost is sidekicks. "Batman and Robin" is a phrase that has permeated pop culture for nearly eight decades. The Boy Wonder has been at Batman's side since 1940. Debuting in *Detective Comics* #38, Robin was created by Bob Kane, Bill Finger, and Jerry Robinson in order to attract younger readers. He brought colorful and youthful energy to Batman's dark world and a phenomenon was born.

Despite several characters bearing the mantle of "Robin" over the years, the original is still the most well-known and beloved. Dick Grayson was an acrobat in the circus alongside his parents. Together they were the Flying Graysons, the main attraction in Haley's Circus. One afternoon a man named Tony Zucco is thrown out of the circus's main office for trying to hustle "insurance." Of course, it's in reality an extortion scam and Zucco leaves angrily, promising that they'll regret it. The following night during the Flying Graysons' act, there is a fatal accident on the trapeze cords. Dick, along with the entire audience, witnesses his parents tumble to their deaths. The police investigate and discover that the trapeze wires were tampered with. Dick points them towards Zucco and the police decide he needs a safe house and protection. Bruce Wayne approaches them and offers to take the boy. He had also been in the audience and Bruce knows all too well the pain and anguish that Dick feels. Soon, Batman is hot on the trail of Zucco and also discovers that Dick has been tracking Zucco as well. Dick endangers himself in the process and so Batman decides to reveal his identity to Dick and take him on as both sidekick and heir.

By adoption, Bruce brought Dick Grayson into his world and that meant that Dick got to partake in everything Bruce had. It is the same for us when we become a follower of Christ. By being born again, we become an adopted son of God and heirs to the Kingdom of Heaven. "He predestined us for adoption to Himself as sons through Jesus Christ, according to the purpose of His will," Paul wrote in Ephesians 1:5 (ESV). Through the death and resurrection of Jesus, we become not only heirs but His sidekicks as well. Essentially we become the Robin to God's Batman. We are to help God in His missions throughout the earth. Oftentimes, this may be very intimidating but Paul also wrote in Romans 8:15 (ESV), "For you did not receive the spirit of slavery to fall back into fear, but you have received the Spirit of adoption as sons, by whom we cry, 'Abba! Father!'" It is not a curse but a privilege to be the sidekicks and heir of the greatest Hero.

This isn't the only lesson to be learned from Robin though. In "Robin's Reckoning, Parts 1 & 2" Tony Zucco was never initially captured by Batman and evaded the police for many years before resurfacing again in Gotham. Living under an assumed name, Zucco is in hiding and Batman finally picks up the trail once more. Robin discovers this himself though and is angry that Batman didn't include him.

"You deceived me!" Robin cries irately.

Batman responds sternly, "Sorry, Robin, but on this team I call the shots."

At the end of part two, Robin finally has his parents' killer in his hands, rage pumping through his body when Batman tells him to stand down. "Stuff your advice, Batman! You and your stone cold heart! You don't know how I feel! How could you?" Robin shouts back but then suddenly realizes what he has said. Robin apologizes and comments on how

Batman must have known that he would let his emotions get the better of him and that's why Batman tried to keep him off the case. Batman replies that it wasn't that at all. He simply was afraid of Zucco destroying the last of the Grayson family and didn't want to lose Robin too.

It is often the same between us and our adoptive Father. We scream at God that He deceives us when we don't get what we think is ours. God then reminds us that on this team, He calls the shots. We may even accuse Him of being cold-hearted and not understanding how we feel. Then like Robin, we sheepishly apologize and realize the folly of such an attitude. God knows exactly what we need, when we need it, and knows how we feel. Jesus put on skin and came down here to see exactly how we feel. In the end His main motivation for protecting us, reprimanding us, or teaching us is the same as Batman's for Robin. He loves us and holds us dear. That's what we get as His adopted sons and daughters.

So let's stick with what He asks of us. When God is with us, we make an even better team than Batman and Robin!

MAD HATTER

The Mad Hatter is one of the more obscure villains Batman has tussled with over the years. First appearing in 1948, the Mad Hatter was another gimmick character who often was only motivated by headwear in his crimes. The Mad Hatter, whose real name is Jervis Tetch, became more fleshed out in various comics in the ensuing decades. On October 12, 1992, "Mad as a Hatter" aired and gave him some emotional depth.

Tetch is working as a scientist for Wayne Industries. His experiments revolve around technology that promises to unlock the human mind. He is clearly unhappy in his job, wallowing in a one-sided love affair with the receptionist, ironically named Alice. Tetch's supervisor, Marcia Cates, is unnecessarily tough on him. His research is not ready to be shared with Bruce and Cates comes down on him hard for it, in spite of Bruce graciously giving him all the time that he needs. Tetch's concerns only go back to Alice, however, and he delights upon discovering that she broke up with her boyfriend. He devises a plot to win her heart and it involves utilizing his budding mind control technology.

Tetch puts on a garish suit and top hat (reminiscent of his *Alice in Wonderland* counterpart) and brings Alice out for a night on the town. He has secretly planted his mind-control cards on numerous people. He is able to thwart a mugging in the park. Photographers stop the couple for a photo opportunity. The head chef gives them special treatment. Their night ends with a walk through a fantasy-themed amusement park featuring an *Alice in Wonderland* section. It's a night to remember for Tetch but his emotional high is dashed the following day. He discovers that Alice's boyfriend returned, apologized for their earlier fight, and proposed to Alice. This news sends Tetch into a jealous rage and he soon kidnaps Dr. Cates, Alice's fiancé, and some thugs for protection. All are under Tetch's control and he plans on forcing Alice to be with him. Tetch even goes so far as to use his technology on Alice herself.

Jealousy and envy are amongst the most difficult of sinful traps to stay out of. The Enemy can use our heart's desire to tempt us and turn us into monsters like the Mad Hatter. These are serious enough sins that God made them part of the Ten Commandments. Exodus 20:17 (ESV) says, "You shall not covet your neighbor's wife." We cannot covet and lust after someone else as Tetch does towards Alice. This merely creates strife between us and others. Tetch no longer loved Alice, he merely wanted her like a possession. 1 Corinthians 13:4 (ESV) says, "Love is patient and kind; love does not envy or boast; it is not arrogant." All these are what became of Jervis Tetch. If he truly loved Alice, he would not treat her like something he was owed.

Tetch retreats with Alice into the heart of the theme park where their date had ended the previous night. He recreates the famous tea party scene with Alice sitting helplessly at the head of the table. Batman confronts them there and Tetch angrily tells Batman that he's waited all his life for her. Batman responds, "Then all you've waited for is a puppet; a soulless little doll!" Tetch was driven to do the one thing that God Himself would never do to us. He does not force us to love Him. God gave us free will and we can choose to turn to Him or not. He is not interested in a lifeless doll who does not have the choice to love Him. God does not turn us into what Tetch turned Alice into. He wants our love to be genuine. He wants us to love Him of our own accord and not be forced into it. Otherwise, our love would mean nothing.

Batman, of course, is able to defeat the Mad Hatter and Alice is freed from her trance. She sees her fiancé and they are reunited in true love. Turn to God and feel the same bond!

Batman: Mask of the Phantasm

BRUCE WAYNE

The beloved animated film *Mask of the Phantasm* is popular for many reasons, one being the territory the film explores that is not seen in the animated series. The series does not spend a lot of time on Bruce Wayne as a young adult just prior to becoming Batman. The creators used the animated film as an opportunity to explore this time in his life. We find a young Bruce struggling to put his plan to rid Gotham of crime into action. We don't know how long Bruce has been back home from his travels but it's clear that Batman hasn't come into his mind yet. He often visits his parents' graves and meditates on the plan.

This is where he meets Andrea Beaumont, whom Bruce forms a relationship with. He catches Andrea talking aloud to her own mother's grave and at first he doesn't realize to whom she is speaking. They begin discussing their respective parents and Andrea asks Bruce what he says to them. He replies that he made a secret vow and declines to get into it further. That secret vow though, of course, is to save Gotham from the evil that took his parents' lives and Bruce soon realizes how difficult it is to keep.

His first night of crime fighting does not go well. Bruce goes out into the streets wearing only a ski mask and a leather jacket; his only weapons are a few throwing stars and spiked ball bearings. His first heroic act is stopping a warehouse theft. Naturally, the thieves only mock him and while Bruce does take most of them down, he endangers the life of a security guard and allows one of the crooks to get away. Bruce chases as the straggler tries to get away in a tractor trailer. The police follow and it ends in a huge crash. Bruce is fortunate to escape with his life and is also lucky that no one was killed due to his recklessness. Still, he is encouraged but also realizes his biggest problem – they weren't afraid of him.

Bruce's frustrations only grow as his attraction to Andrea grows as well. The more serious their relationship gets, the more unrealistic the plan seems to him. Bruce feels he can't risk his life every night with Andrea waiting for him to come home. But Bruce made a vow and he is greatly conflicted. He finds himself pleading with the specter of his parents at their tombstone, imploring them to release him from his promise. He says that he can give money to the police instead and help in other ways. Andrea arrives, saying maybe his parents sent her as a sign; they embrace each other. Unfortunately, Andrea later mysteriously ends their engagement just a day after Bruce proposes. He then has no reason not to keep his vow to his parents and thus Batman is born.

Are you a man of your word? Do you follow through on something when you say that you're going to do it? Or do people have no expectation of you coming through? God takes vows extremely seriously. "If a man vows a vow to the Lord, or swears an oath to bind himself by a pledge, he shall not break his word. He shall do according to all that proceeds out of his mouth," it says in Numbers 30:2 (ESV). When God says He will do something, you can be sure that God does it (Numbers 23:19). He wants us to be just as reliable and accountable to one another. Ecclesiastes 5:4-5 (ESV) says, "When you vow a vow to God, do not delay paying it, for He has no pleasure in fools. Pay what you vow. It is better that you should not than that you should vow and not pay." In other words, don't make promises you can't keep! It will make you look foolish to others and teach them that you can't be trusted. Jesus gave simple advice regarding vows as well. "Let what you say be simply 'Yes' or 'No'; anything more than this comes from evil," He said in Matthew 5:37 (ESV). Don't overcomplicate things by promising more than you can deliver. You only let others down and ruin your reputation!

THOMAS WAYNE

T he relationship between father and son is something that is at the heart of humanity. This is so because it stems from our great Creator and His Son. Therefore, it informs much of our lives and subsequently much of our fiction as well. It is a relationship that is integral to the story of Bruce Wayne. Christopher Nolan's *Batman Begins* is one of the best depictions of the relationship between Bruce and his father Thomas Wayne.

Played in the film by Linus Roache, Thomas Wayne is a very successful surgeon whose skills were parlayed into a fruitful company. Thomas embodies compassion and intelligence and sets an example for his son of how to use these gifts to help other people. Thomas carries the family's wealth humbly, telling Bruce that he leaves the company in the hands of "more interested men." One of his chief contributions to Gotham is the central train station that travels throughout the city. He explains to Bruce that Gotham has been good to their family and they wanted to repay the city by building affordable transportation for everyone.

Bruce's father served as inspiration too in his darkest moments. The opening scene of the film portrays Bruce falling through an old well and down a shaft on the Wayne property. Bruce is attacked by several bats and is horrified until he sees his father rappelling down above him. Thomas reaches out and grabs Bruce by the hand. He then hoists themselves up and into the light. "Why do we fall, Bruce? So we can learn to pick ourselves back up," Thomas tells Bruce. It is one of the film's recurring themes and a repeated line of dialogue. Bruce uses this to motivate himself throughout all of his obstacles and even Alfred echoes this sentiment when Bruce is at his weakest.

Why do we fall? Why does God allow the good to suffer? Why must we go through unpleasant circumstances? No one knows for sure why tragedies strike certain people. However, we know God doesn't let these things go unnoticed. Psalms 56:8 (ESV) says, "You have kept count of my tossings; put my tears in your bottle. Are they not in your book?" God keeps track of every tear shed and will not allow a single one to go to waste.

Thomas's remark to Bruce is reminiscent of 1 Peter 1:7 (NLT), "These trials will show that your faith is genuine. It is being tested as fire tests and purifies gold – though your faith is far more precious than mere gold. So when your faith remains strong through many trials, it will bring you much praise and glory and honor on the day when Jesus Christ is revealed to the whole world." We fall so that we can learn. We fall so that we can become stronger for having the experience. We fall so that our Father can pick us up and He is glorified. He does this out of His love for us too.

We all find ourselves in dark places like Bruce did when he was in that shaft. When the Enemy is coming at us from the shadowy places, we can look up and see God rappelling down to get us. We just have to reach up and grasp His hand. He will lift us out and into the light.

Batman Begins

BRUCE WAYNE

B ruce Wayne began his life as a young boy permanently scarred by the
tragic murder of his parents. This single event that he witnessed sent
him on a trip around the world in search of strength, power, and purpose.
Ultimately, Bruce returned to Gotham with all of these and with the help
of a few Wayne Enterprises prototypes, Bruce creates his new persona –
the Batman.

Bruce's thirst for justice is channeled into the personality of his
creation, but Batman had to be more than just a man and more than a
vigilante. This has been portrayed in various iterations. In *Batman Begins,*
Bruce first approaches Jim Gordon in just his prototype suit and a ski
mask. A near fatal fall triggers his research into a gliding solution. Thus
the cape is added. In *Batman: Mask of the Phantasm,* Bruce's first attempt
at fighting crime nearly ends disastrously. Wearing only a ski mask and a
leather jacket, Bruce tries to break up a smuggling ring. Needless to say,
it does not go according to plan. The criminals merely mock Bruce and
open fire on him, endangering a hostage and the police. In Frank Miller
and David Mazzucchelli's *Batman: Year One,* upon returning to Gotham,
Bruce irresponsibly ventures out into the worst Gotham neighborhood
and gets into a deadly brawl in regular clothes.

In every incarnation, Bruce realizes he needs better tools and a fearsome persona to rid Gotham City of crime. So what goes into Batman's arsenal? He has his armored suit, his cape and cowl, and of course the renowned utility belt. The belt itself has weapons and tools, from the famous batarangs to the infamous sharp repellant (*Batman: The Movie* with Adam West). These are the things that aid Batman in performing his heroic feats, to rescue those in need, and fight evil.

Most superheroes are often portrayed as being ordinary outside of their costumes or armor. Part of the appeal is the idea we can become something more and can perform these huge displays of power ourselves. Bruce Wayne slips on his cowl and becomes the Dark Knight, Clark Kent tears open his everyday clothing to reveal his Superman shield underneath, and we watch and dream in awe and aspire to change ourselves into something grander as well.

How great is it then to be able to don the Armor of God and do exactly that? God graciously affords us our own devices to perform feats of heroism for His Kingdom. While they may not be a literal cape and cowl and we don't get an actual utility belt, God's Armor is far more effective in our everyday lives. Paul wrote in Ephesians, 6:11 (ESV) "Put on the whole armor of God, that you may be able to stand against the schemes of the devil."

What is in this arsenal? The Belt of Truth, which will protect against Satan's lies; the Breastplate of Righteousness, to defend your heart against temptation; the Shoes of Peace, to move you to spread the Good News; the Shield of Faith, "with which you can extinguish all the flaming darts of the evil one" (Ephesians 6:16 ESV); the Helmet of Salvation, which will keep your mind safe from doubt and other mental attacks, and finally the Sword of the Spirit, "which is the word of God" (Ephesians 6:18 ESV).

These are the items that will allow us to do great things. This is so because we aren't relying on our own power. We can only do things through God's power. The truth is we don't have Bruce Wayne's resources or the time to travel the world and train like he did as a young man. Besides that, he is mortal and fallible just as any of us. True power comes from God Almighty, Who is more than willing to share His power. Jesus said, "For apart from me you can do nothing," (John 15:5 ESV). He also reminded the disciples, "With man this is impossible, but with God all things are possible," (Matthew 19:26 ESV).

God can enable us to be superheroes and do great things through us but we need to use His Armor and rely on His power. It worked with people like David, the disciples, and it can with you as well.

RA'S AL GHUL

Ra's al Ghul was introduced into Batman's world in June 1971 by editor Julius Schwartz, writer Dennis O'Neil, and artist Neal Adams, thus making Ra's one of the "newest" of Batman's rogue's gallery. However, Ra's has also proven to be one of the most popular and lasting villains. An environmental extremist, his driving motivation is the purification of the earth and his disdain for humanity. Ra's is the leader of the League of Assassins and his name is loosely translated into "The Demon's Head."

Prior to 2005, Ra's had not been portrayed in a live-action film and had only been adapted for *Batman: The Animated Series*. That changed though when Christopher Nolan and David Goyer were conceiving *Batman Begins*. In the film, Bruce Wayne is rotting away in a prison in South Asia when he's confronted by a man named Henri Ducard, played by Liam Neeson. This man pays Bruce's bail and challenges him to find Ra's al Ghul's headquarters in the mountains. Bruce eventually finds them and meets the supposed Ra's, played by Ken Watanabe. In order to finish his training, Bruce is ordered by Ra's to execute a prisoner who has been charged with murdering his neighbor. Bruce refuses, creates a diversion that eventually causes a huge explosion, and fights Ra's al Ghul, who is crushed under fiery debris. Bruce knocks Ducard unconscious and leaves him safely in the nearby town. At the climax of the film, we discover that

Ducard was in fact just a moniker and that he is in reality Ra's al Ghul. He begins to explain to Bruce how his League of Shadows has fought injustice throughout the decades in various cities and now it's Gotham's turn to be destroyed.

The depiction of Ra's in *Batman Begins* differs slightly from the version seen in comics and animation in this sense: he is not as concerned with the planet as much as he is justice and balance. When he is training Bruce under the guise of Ducard, Ra's explains to Bruce that only vengeance will bring him peace (which we as Christ followers know is a lie). Ra's tells the story of how he lost his wife, how she was taken from him, and how only vengeance stopped his pain and anger.

Later when Bruce insists that the prisoner he is ordered to kill deserves a fair trial, Ra's is appalled. "Criminals mock society's laws! You know this better than most!"

In the climax of the film, Ra's reveals himself at Bruce's birthday party. Bruce says in disbelief of Ra's hostility, "I saved your life."

"I warned you about compassion," Ra's says coldly. He then goes onto explain his motivation for destroying Gotham. "Crime, despair; this is not how man was meant to live." Ra's utterly rejects Bruce's plea for more time to help Gotham overcome its criminal element.

What does it mean to be completely just? We know that only God Almighty is perfect in His justice. God cannot tolerate sin and seeks to eradicate it from our lives with the swiftness of Ra's al Ghul. Deuteronomy 16:19 ESV says, "You shall not pervert justice. You shall not show partiality, and you shall not accept a bribe, for a bribe blinds the eyes of the wise and subverts the cause of the righteous." This certainly sounds like Ra's attitude towards the criminality of Gotham. We have also seen God's wrath towards rebellion, sin, and disobedience many times in the Old Testament, particularly when dealing with Sodom and Gomora (Genesis 19). But we also know God to be full of love, grace, and patience (Hebrews 4:16; Romans 3:24). He gave up His only Son to save us (John 3:16-17). So what is God without His mercy, love, and grace? Ra's al Ghul, who only thirsts for his idea of justice and vengeance.

Oftentimes, we can be like Ra's. We forget that God's forgiveness applies to everyone and that we are called to pray for wrongdoers (Luke 6:35). Too often, Christians can walk around and click their tongues at people whom they judge to be less than them. But we all fall short and we shouldn't be quick to punish others for their sins like Ra's.

It's true what Ra's says to Bruce, that this is "not how man was meant to live." However, Ra's isn't God and neither are we. It is the Lord's job to eventually set things right and we know that He will (Revelation 22: 1-5). Instead of being like Ra's al Ghul, follow Bruce's example. Don't tolerate sin but ask God for help shining His light into people's lives and show them the way.

"No, O people, the Lord has told you what is good, and this is what he requires of you: to do what is right, to love mercy, and to walk humbly with your God," Micah 6:8 (NLT).

Batman Begins

RACHEL DAWES

Rachel Dawes is an original character introduced in Christopher Nolan's Batman trilogy. First played by Katie Holmes in *Batman Begins,* Rachel is a childhood friend of Bruce Wayne. We are introduced to them in the opening scene of the film when they are playing in the Wayne Manor garden. It is there that Bruce falls into the cave and develops his fear of bats.

Years after the death of the Waynes, Rachel has worked her way up the Gotham legal system. She is an assistant district attorney and helping D.A. Finch to incriminate Carmine Falcone. Bruce returns to Gotham after being away at college because the murderer of Thomas and Martha Wayne, Joe Chill, is testifying against Falcone. However, things go awry when Chill is murdered outside the courthouse. An argument between Rachel and Bruce ensues and he then disappears, venturing on the trip that trains him to eventually become Batman.

Seven years pass until Rachel and Bruce see each other face to face again, during which Bruce has been declared legally dead. Days after Bruce's return to Gotham is made public, they run into each other in a hotel lobby. Rachel is just arriving and Bruce is leaving with his two dates for the evening, a pair of European models. Bruce is fully into his "billionaire playboy" persona, as suggested by Alfred to throw off any suspicions that he may be the Batman. When he sees Rachel however, suddenly the façade cracks slightly.

"It's been a long time," Rachel says in disbelief. She asks Bruce, who is soaked from an impromptu dip in the hotel fountain, why he's all wet.

"Swimming," he oddly responds and then asks how the job is going.

Rachel replies that it's getting worse in Gotham and remarks that Bruce is too busy "swimming" to help her.

Bruce, feeling ashamed, tries to convince her, "Rachel, all of this, it's not me inside. I am more."

Rachel looks at him skeptically and utters one of the film's more memorable lines. "It's not who are you underneath, it's what you *do* that defines you."

It's a truth that can resonate with all of us and one that can even be found in the Word as well. James wrote about this very thing in chapter two of his letter. Without works, faith is dead. As Rachel points out to Bruce, you may be a great person underneath and believe in Jesus, but without doing anything with that knowledge, what good is your faith? "You believe that there is one God. You do well. Even the demons believe – and tremble!" (James 2:19 NKJV). We must put our faith into action by obeying the things that the Bible says and helping to build the Kingdom. Jesus taught the disciples to teach and serve others, to love their neighbors and their enemies. Jesus also told them, "Go therefore and make disciples of all nations, baptizing them in the name of the Father and of the Son and of the Holy Spirit" (Matthew 28:18 ESV). These are the things we must do as well. Otherwise, what good is it to say that we have faith?

Essentially, if Bruce had come back to Gotham after those seven years, to a city that was much worse than when he had left and done nothing with the skills he acquired, what good would he be? That's what Rachel tried to impart upon him. Later when she asks Batman for his real name and he repeats the phrase she used earlier, Rachel realizes who Batman really is and sees Bruce's inner qualities at work. It is the same with us. God gave up Jesus so we would be saved by our faith in Him but also to perform good works also. We can't just sit on our salvation. As Paul wrote,

"For it is not the hearers of the law who are righteous before God, but the doers of the law who will be justified" (Romans 2:13 ESV).

"For as the body apart from the spirit is dead, so also faith apart from works is dead," James 2:26 ESV.

The Dark Knight

TWO-FACE

I n the second film of Christopher Nolan's Batman trilogy, Harvey Dent is taking Gotham City by storm. He is a media darling and beloved by the people for both his charming smile and body of work. Imagine a politician or public servant who is actually doing what he promised. The streets are cleaner than ever and as Bruce Wayne says to Rachel at one point, Dent does it "without wearing a mask." Gotham is smitten with their new, dashing district attorney. It is understandable, given the people's experiences beforehand with corrupt government and cops on the take. Batman's presence has weeded out corruption and allowed someone like Dent to take office. Bruce even begins to hope that perhaps his alter ego will no longer be needed in Gotham.

Nevertheless, things quickly go awry after the Joker appears and starts wreaking havoc across the city. The worst thing Joker does is bring Gotham's white knight, Harvey Dent, down to his level. After disfiguring Harvey and pushing him to the brink of insanity, Dent finally snaps and goes on his own revenge-fueled crime spree. Jim Gordon and his unit frantically try to find Dent before the public find out what has happened to their DA. Ultimately, Dent is killed in a fall while making an attempt on the lives of Gordon's family. The people's hopes are hinged so greatly on Dent that Gordon fears their hopes will be permanently squashed.

Their faith in the system will be irrevocably broken and there will be no fixing their city. In the end, Batman sacrifices his own reputation and takes the blame both for Dent's death and crimes so that Dent's standing will remain pristine.

It can be easy to hang our hopes on people who are charismatic and seem trustworthy. They may even genuinely be those things and have the greatest intentions in the world. Nevertheless, the truth is we are human and we sin. We frequently fail and come up short. We let one another down and it can often be quite painful and disappointing. It is like that for Gotham and Harvey Dent. He was essentially their idol and idols are always destined to be failures. Idols are anything that takes the place of God, anything that we worship like Him, anything that we devote our time to. It is also anything that we place our hopes in instead of God. He detests idols (Leviticus 26:1).

God detests idols because He is the one, true, and sovereign God. He wants to be recognized for who He is and deserves the glory for it because of His goodness. God is goodness, love, mercy, and grace incarnate. No idol can replicate his qualities. Idols are dangerous because they take God's rightful position in our lives. They can be anything from human leaders like Harvey Dent to our marriages, work, hobbies, celebrities, athletes, or possessions. Even we ourselves can be our own idols. The ancient Israelites were constantly putting their faith in other cultures' false gods.

In the Old Testament days, most idols were fictional deities who were represented by carved stones or metal structures. Clearly, Dent was a living person but any human being that is held to such a high standard can also be an idol. If you put that kind of expectation or hope in a person, they will inevitably disappoint you. Even Bane refers to Harvey Dent as a "fallen idol" in *The Dark Knight Rises*.

When you put your faith in other people or things above Almighty God, you will suffer disastrous spiritual consequences. You will lose your sense of kinship with the Lord and soon your peace will follow. This is what the Enemy wants; to steal our peace and our joy. If we put ourselves in God's position or anyone else, then everything will fall apart.

There's only One who is worth putting your trust into and that's Jesus Christ. He will never let you down. "He committed no sin, neither was deceit found in His mouth," says 1 Peter 2:22 (ESV). Jesus is worthy of your trust, your hopes, and your life. He will never let you down like Dent did Gotham. Otherwise, you will be depending on people and things with no power at all or dependability at all. Isaiah 57:13 says, "When you cry out, let your collection of idols deliver you! The wind will carry them all off, a breath will take them away. But he who takes refuge in me shall possess the land and shall inherit my holy mountain."

The Dark Knight

THE JOKER

In the second of Christopher Nolan's Batman trilogy, the late Heath Ledger plays the iconic villain the Joker. In a truly landmark performance that earned him a posthumous Academy Award, Ledger brought the most infamous villain in comics to life in a way that is truly chilling.

The Joker, both in this specific film and in the comics, represents humanity at its absolute lowest. He is a character that simply embodies depravity and hopelessness, with a total disdain for life. While the Joker has had various origins and backgrounds in comics throughout the years, in *The Dark Knight* he is not given any such definitive origin. The Joker is simply the antithesis of everything Batman stands for. He is the total and opposite reaction of evil to what Bruce Wayne does with his Batman persona. Such is the "escalation" that Jim Gordon warns Batman about at the end of previous film.

After the Joker's first attempt on Harvey Dent's life, Bruce Wayne is in his bunker trying to find the primary motive behind this new threat. He remarks to Alfred that criminals aren't complicated and that they just have to find out what the Joker wants. But Alfred tells Bruce that perhaps he is the one who doesn't understand. Alfred explains that some men aren't looking for anything logical like money, saying, "Some men just want to watch the world burn."

It is this line of dialogue that conjures up John 10:10 (ESV).

"The thief comes only to steal and kill and destroy. I came that they may have life and have it abundantly," Jesus says.

Satan has rebelled against God since before creation and his only motivation has been destruction, suffering, envy, and evil. Much like the Joker's disdain for life and happiness, the Enemy only wants to take from us that which makes us joyful. Whatever good Batman, Jim Gordon, and Harvey Dent were doing to clean up the streets of Gotham, the Joker undid. Likewise, Satan tries to tear down the efforts of Christians and our God. However, we know that Satan has already lost (Revelation 20:10).

Perhaps the centerpiece of the film is a scene in which Batman is sitting across from the Joker in an interrogation room. It is this scene that exemplifies the thematic struggle between hero and villain. Joker tells Batman that the moral code of the cops and the city is a bad joke. He contends that the so-called civilized people will eat each other at the first sign of trouble. Later in the scene, Joker tells Batman "the only way to live in this world is without rules." Such is the lie that the Enemy has been telling mankind since he convinced Adam and Eve to eat the forbidden fruit. Do what you want says the Enemy, don't bother to follow God's laws (Genesis 3:1-5).

After Joker and his men have murdered Rachel Dawes and have disfigured Harvey Dent, he confronts Dent in his hospital room. It is here that the Joker tricks Harvey into succumbing to darkness and anger, telling him that only chaos is truly fair. Joker has utter contempt for Jim Gordon, Gotham's mayor, and anyone who keeps order. He snidely refers to them as "schemers." Joker refers to himself as an "agent of chaos." This is how the Enemy operates as well and it is the total opposite of God. Paul wrote in 1 Corinthians 14:33 (ESV), "For God is not a God of confusion but of peace."

Joker brags about how he took Harvey Dent's plan and turned it on its head. Then by goading Dent further and further, he pushes Harvey into his Two-Face persona. Two-Face then goes on his vengeance-fueled killing spree and dies in an attempt on Jim Gordon's son's life. Gordon laments how they wasted any chance Batman gave them of rescuing Gotham from despair. Ultimately, Batman takes the blame for Dent's crimes so that Joker loses and Gotham can retain its hope.

Maybe this is how Satan felt when he ruined paradise and Adam and Eve were thrown out into the world. The devil saw God's plans for His creation and so he turned them upside down. Or so he thought. Little did the devil know that God ultimately had a plan to undo the damage that was done. Much like how Batman sacrificed his reputation to protect Gotham from the Joker's gambit, Jesus, our Hero, came to undo the damage Satan did that day in Eden. By becoming the ultimate sacrifice for sin, Jesus gave us everlasting hope, conquered Satan and his power over death. God through His one and only Son defeated the agent of chaos and has given us everlasting hope.

Two-Face

In *The Dark Knight*, Aaron Eckhart plays Harvey Dent, the dashing new district attorney in Gotham City. He has quickly become a force for good and an enemy to the criminal underworld. Unflappable, Dent even remains calm when a suspect on the witness stand tries to shoot him in the middle of a trial.

You would think that such a man would make for an obvious and immediate ally for Jim Gordon and Batman, but that isn't the case at first. Both are suspicious of Dent and given the level of corruption in the office's past, their distrust is understandable. The first meeting that Dent and Gordon have is cautious and at times combative. Dent asks Gordon where he's been able to acquire lightly irradiated bills for tracking the mob's money. When Gordon makes an unconvincing reference to "various agencies" Dent gets annoyed and insists on meeting Batman, of whom he approves. Gordon also gets defensive when Dent accuses Gordon's unit of being full of dirty cops. Eventually, the pair of them settle things and decide to cooperate with one another.

Dent insists on having Gordon's trust, to which Gordon responds, "You don't have to sell me, Dent. We all know you're Gotham's white knight."

Dent chuckles and says he's heard they have a different name for him in Gordon's department. "I wouldn't know about that," Gordon sheepishly replies.

Later in the film after Rachel Dawes has been killed by the Joker and Dent has been horribly disfigured, we find out just what the nickname is. Gordon goes to see Dent in the hospital, who is both physically and emotionally scarred. Dent demands that Gordon utter the nickname they had given him – Harvey Two-Face. Gordon can barely look at Dent, who has become a physical manifestation of the nickname, the right side of his face bearing charred skin and exposed muscle.

Nobody likes a hypocrite. Is there anything more aggravating than someone who says one thing and does another? People who claim to be Christians must walk the walk and not just talk the talk. Know who else doesn't like hypocrisy? Jesus Himself. "How can you say to your brother, 'Brother, let me take out the speck that is in your eye,' when you yourself do not see the log that is in your own eye? You hypocrite, first take the log out of your own eye, and then you will see clearly to take the speck that is in your brother's eye," Luke 6:42 (ESV). Jesus often battled the Pharisees for acting pious but secretly being full of sin and corruption themselves.

Surely we've all met people who act high and mighty but in actuality do all the things they scold other people for. These are the Harvey Two-Faces of the world. When you allow yourself to garner attention and a lofty reputation but in reality don't live up to it, people will give you unflattering nicknames and mock you. For all of Harvey Dent's righteousness, he was secretly as vicious as the criminals he was trying to bring down. The bitterness he shows towards Gordon in the end eventually turns into true evil as he kidnaps Gordon's family as punishment for Rachel's death. In the end, Dent was far from a white knight.

Follow in Jesus's steps and have integrity as a true follower of His. Don't be Two-Faced.

BRUCE WAYNE

I magine dedicating fifteen years of your life to something only to see it come crashing down. Worse yet, what if you dedicated all those years to something and then it ended? What would your life revolve around then? Such an empty place is where we find Bruce Wayne at the start of *The Dark Knight Rises*.

Eight years earlier, Batman took the fall for Harvey Dent and Gotham has been virtually crime free ever since. But for Bruce Wayne, the victory has been hollow and come at a price. Searching for other ways to help the world after hanging up his cape and cowl, Bruce poured his fortune into a fusion reactor in an effort to develop clean energy. Unfortunately, research performed by a Russian scientist created the possibility of turning Bruce's reactor into a hydrogen bomb (and this is exactly what Bane eventually does later in the film). Bruce shutters the entire project and his public image along with it. The failure of the clean energy project combined with the loss of Rachel Dawes from years earlier crushes Bruce.

So Bruce Wayne has not been seen for years now. During a public function at Wayne Manor, catering staff whisper to each other about the "crazy guy" who owns the house. Bruce has essentially become Howard Hughes, a mythical figure whom is rarely seen by anyone. Bearded and still limping from the fall he took at the end of *The Dark Knight*, Bruce lives in a secluded wing of Wayne Manor, interacting only with Alfred. Much of the manor is covered over with sheets and tarps, resembling a mausoleum (and is a callback to the look of the Manor in *Batman Begins* following the death of the Waynes).

It is only after his first encounter with Selina Kyle that Bruce begins to come out of his shell in any way at all. Much to Alfred's dismay, he finds Bruce in the cave, commenting that Bruce hasn't been down there in a long time. Bruce is running background checks on Selina and Alfred cracks a joke about the two exchanging tips over coffee. Alfred becomes more serious, imploring Bruce to try to "find a life beyond that awful cave."

Their relationship only worsens as Bruce learns of Bane and the threat that this masked terrorist presents to Gotham City. True, this news motivates Bruce to find a solution for his limp and to go out into the city once more, but Alfred only worries further. "You can strap up your leg and put your mask back on but that doesn't make you what you were," Alfred lectures.

"You're afraid that if I go back out there, I'll fail," Bruce accuses him.

Alfred simply responds, "No. I'm afraid that you want to."

When Bruce returns from Batman's first night back, he and Alfred have another argument. This time it results in Bruce admitting the real reason he can't move on with his life – Rachel. The way he sees it, he can't move on because Rachel didn't get the same chance to move on also. However, Alfred counters by finally revealing that he had hidden the truth from Bruce – that Rachel chose Harvey Dent over him. The two lifelong friends part ways and suddenly Bruce has lost everything: Alfred, Rachel, his parents; all he's left with is Batman.

We're all in search of purpose in this life. We were created with one purpose in mind, which is fellowship with God. Without Him, we're left with a massive void inside that nothing else can fill. People can try to fill it with many things. People think their romantic relationships will satisfy them; they think their careers are their life purpose. It can be wealth, pleasure, or any number of things. But the truth is that these will all let you down at some point. There will either come a point where they no longer feel fulfilling or they will simply end. It is no different than where we find Bruce at this point in his life. Without Rachel and Batman, his life had no purpose. His one other attempt, the clean energy project, failed miserably. Then he rushed back into his alter ego to fulfill that void again.

Only Jesus can fill that void though. The type of thirst that Bruce felt can only be quenched by the Son of God. "But whoever drinks of the water that I will give him will never be thirsty again. The water that I will give him will become in him a spring of water welling up to eternal life," John 4:14 (ESV). Jesus can fill every desire, need, and want that we have. He is dependable and trustworthy. We know that He lasts forever (Revelation 22:14). So there's no chance that you're investing your life in something that will fail you, run out, or just be temporary. Even the most heroic of us needs the rock solid foundation of Jesus Christ.

The Dark Knight Rises

CATWOMAN

The past can often be a very haunting thing. We all make choices in our lives that have varying effects on us and those around us. Sometimes, these choices can result in pain, embarrassment, or tragedy. A person can feel marked by decisions they've made or mistakes that they just can't seem to shake. We live in a world where our record often defines us and marks us. All we want sometimes is a fresh start. A clean slate.

This is where we find Selina Kyle in *The Dark Knight Rises,* Christopher Nolan's capper on his Batman trilogy. Played by Anne Hathaway, Selina is a hardened cat burglar and grifter, who is looking for a way out of her life. Bruce Wayne first encounters her in Wayne Manor, where she is posing as one of the maids so that can she crack a safe in his bedroom. After doing more research about her, Bruce discovers the details of her sordid past and tracks her down to a charity ball where Selina is swindling rich Gothamites. Her justification for stealing is simple – you can't outrun your past. Bruce suggests starting fresh to which Selina scoffs, "There are no fresh starts in today's world. A 12-year-old with a cell phone can find out what you did."

For much of the movie, Selina's motivation is finding the Clean Slate, an alleged software program that can completely erase any and all documentation regarding a person and his or her legal background. It's this program that Selina sees as her way out of the life she's chosen for herself. Yet, the software proves too elusive to acquire. Selina only digs herself deeper trying to find it and becomes a pawn for John Daggett and Bane. After breaking into Daggett's office looking for it, he taunts her and tells her it was a gangland myth; it simply doesn't exist.

As for the rest of us in the real world, we may not be world class jewel thieves but we all need a clean slate. The good news is that our clean slate isn't found in a near-mythical software program but in faith in Jesus Christ. This fresh start is made available to us through Jesus's death and resurrection. By taking on the punishment for our sins, we are made clean in the eyes of God. Isaiah 1:18 (ESV) says, "Though your sins are like scarlet, they shall be as white as snow; though they are red like crimson, they shall become like wool."

This is the new beginning that Selina Kyle is looking for and it isn't just a matter of erasing your history from government records. You can become a brand new person entirely. Paul wrote in 2 Corinthians 5:17 (ESV), "Therefore, if anyone is in Christ, he is a new creation. The old has passed away; behold the new has come." Jesus can help take away that past and then point you towards a far better future, all the while helping you become the person He envisions. During the film Bruce Wayne, in and out of costume, repeatedly tells Selina that he senses there's more to her than just her mistakes. Jesus also sees potential in us to do good as well.

In the end, Batman is able to track down the program and is able to help Selina Kyle escape the vicious cycle she found herself in. Our own Hero can do the same for us.

The Dark Knight Rises

JOHN BLAKE

In the finale of Christopher Nolan's Batman trilogy, Joseph Gordon-Levitt played John Blake, a member of the Gotham City Police Department. Young, hotheaded, but also noble and idealistic, he believed in the system and worked hard to maintain peace in Gotham. John Blake was an orphan and had had a rough childhood. His mother died in a car accident when he was a small boy and his father was killed over a gambling debt only a few years later.

It is this pain that helps him identify with Bruce Wayne, whom Blake and his friends at his orphanage admired. They would make up stories about Bruce Wayne, whom they nicknamed "the billionaire orphan." But as Blake explains to Bruce, he recognized the hidden pain underneath the glamor of Bruce's public life. This is how Blake deduced that only Bruce Wayne could have been the Batman.

Months after Batman's disappearance and during Bane's occupation of Gotham, a Special Forces team infiltrates the city and hopes to take down the band of mercenaries. While helping the Special Forces leader track the truck containing Bane's hydrogen bomb, Blake is drawing bat symbols on the city streets. The Special Forces leader scoffs when he notices. "You don't think he's really coming back, do you?"

Blake responds, "It doesn't matter what I think."

"Actually, it does. You should put your faith in something a little more real," the soldier lectures.

This terse exchange between John Blake and the soldier is a great example of something that every Christian is likely to experience at some point in their life. Here is Gotham City under siege by a mad man and this Special Forces captain is working alongside a cop who is expecting to be saved by a guy in a costume. It's ridiculous and absurd to him. But it is the same response we receive to our walk with Jesus. The Christian believer is mocked and receives shakes of the head for placing trust in the fanciful or words in an ancient book. Even in some hero who is supposed to come back and rescue us all, one who is likely dead. But John Blake came to know Batman intimately by spending time with Bruce after their initial encounter. Similarly, we too can know Jesus intimately by spending time in the Word, reading the Gospel, and praying.

So when the rescue efforts of the Special Forces inevitably fail and Blake is about to be executed by Bane's men, his faith is rewarded. Batman swoops down into the fray and makes quick work of the mercenaries. Blake can only look on in wonder and relief. It is the same with us when God bails us out of bad situations or when prayers are answered. He moves quickly and takes down the bad guys and obstacles in our way.

2 Corinthians 5:7 says "for we walk by faith, not by sight" and so we must follow John Blake's example. While our own personal Gotham is under siege, we must draw our symbols on our hearts and wait for our Hero.

The Dark Knight Rises

JIM GORDON

J im Gordon has been one of the most enduring characters in the world of Batman since 1939. Portrayed by Gary Oldman in Nolan's trilogy, Jim Gordon came to Gotham to find a city full of corruption, cops on the take and crooked politicians. It's a thankless and hopeless job but one that he sticks to and does as best he can. Gordon remains one of the few good cops while working alongside hypocrites like Detective Flass, as seen in *Batman Begins*. Of course, things change when a certain costumed vigilante appears and allows Gordon to do his job more effectively.

By the time we see Jim Gordon again in *The Dark Knight Rises*, he has been police commissioner for eight long years. He has spent those eight years carrying the guilt of covering up the crimes of Harvey Dent and moving on in the war against crime without Batman, who has since gone into hiding. As we see on the anniversary of Harvey Dent's death, Gordon toys with the idea of coming clean, even having a speech written down that will reveal the truth of what Two-Face did. Gordon hesitates however and perpetuates the lie.

Bane later steals Gordon's speech and reads it aloud on a TV broadcast to further his agenda that the established order cannot be trusted. Jim Gordon is laying low with John Blake at the time. He is stunned at what's transpiring on the screen. The truth is revealed in the worst possible way that the Harvey Dent Act, which automatically denies parole, was based entirely on a lie. Blake, a firm believer in the Law, is outraged and demands the truth from Gordon.

The Commissioner goes on to explain the desperation he felt in the moment of Dent's death. He talks of how the system failed him time and again, letting the bad guys win, and the Law was no longer a weapon but merely shackles. "One day, you may face a moment of such uncertainty. And when you do, I hope you have a friend like I did. To plunge their hands into the filth so that you can keep yours clean!"

Blake remains unconvinced and says to Gordon, "Your hands look pretty dirty to me, Commissioner."

The Law of God eventually became shackles for the Israelites and by extension, for us too. Paul wrote in Romans 9:31 (NKJV), "But Israel, pursuing the law of righteousness, has not attained to the law of righteousness." While God's law is pure and true, we are not and we become slaves to the law. "Now we know that whatever the law says, it says to those who are under the law, that every mouth may be stopped, and all the world may become guilty before God," says Paul in Romans 3:19 (NKJV). The law's purpose is to show us our inability to be perfect on our own. It is impossible for us to follow these rules to the letter and God knows this. That's why He sent his Son into the world, not to condemn it but to save it (John 3:17). Paul also wrote in Galatians 3:24 (NKJV), "Therefore the law was our tutor to bring us to Christ, that we might be justified by faith."

So Jim Gordon, having become disillusioned by the law that he put his faith in, turned to his friend, Batman, who was willing to take on the punishment and bail Gordon out. While this may have proved foolish and desperate eight years later, our decision to put our faith in Jesus will never turn out that way. He is always willing to plunge his hands into the filth of our sin and failure and pull us out. Jesus will not fail us even when the Enemy accuses us in public, like Bane on the TV broadcast, nor will He look at us with disdain and disappointment like John Blake. Instead, like Batman, He will prove loyal and appear in our weakest moments.

THE JOKER

B atman is a character popular enough that he has been featured in nearly every form of media possible. He has appeared in print, in film, on television, and in video games. Most of the Batman video games that have been published over the years have mostly been pedestrian. It wasn't until 2009 that a video game was finally released that did justice to the character. *Batman: Arkham Asylum,* developed by Rocksteady Studios, features the Dark Knight venturing into the famous madhouse after Joker and other villains break loose and take over. Featuring veteran voice talent from the animated series Kevin Conroy and Mark Hamill and a story by writer Paul Dini, the game was a smash hit. It spawned two sequels and the finale was entitled *Arkham Knight.*

The final game in the series revolves around the Scarecrow unleashing his fear toxin upon Gotham while also exploring the aftermath of the previous entry, *Arkham City,* in which the Joker actually dies. In the beginning of the story, Batman infiltrates Axis Chemicals in an effort to stop the Scarecrow's gas attack. He is only able to marginally limit the explosion and exposes himself to the toxin. Later it is revealed that Batman is also still infected with the Joker's virus (also stemming from *Arkham City*). These two things combined cause Batman to start seeing Joker everywhere. He becomes Batman's invisible companion throughout the game and often taunts, laughs at, or tempts him in various moments. Some of these scenes are played for comedic relief but mostly, they are dramatic and chilling. The Clown Prince's specter often is meant to be discouraging towards Batman and his heroic efforts. Joker effectively becomes the devil on Batman's shoulder.

Satan is always trying to hover over our shoulders and whisper things in our ears. They can be taunts or retorts, they can be discouraging words, or they can be temptations. At any rate, all of Satan's efforts go towards stopping us in our mission for God. The Enemy doesn't want us to be joyful because it motivates us. He also doesn't want us to feel connected to God because He makes us powerful. The devil will do anything to cut off our power and make us weak. Peter said the devil roars like a lion, trying to frighten his prey (1 Peter 5:8).

Did you know that the devil even tried to tempt Jesus? It was just before Jesus began His ministry in Jerusalem. He was fasting in the wilderness for forty days and nights. The devil first attacks Jesus's hungry state by saying, "If you are the Son of God, command these stones to become loaves of bread." Jesus answered, "It is written, 'Man shall not live by bread alone, but by every word that comes from the mouth of God,'" (Matthew 4:2-4 ESV). Then Jesus and the devil are on the highest point of the temple. Satan tries to get Jesus to leap off and force God to send His angels to save Jesus from falling. Jesus responds, "Again it is written, 'You shall not put the Lord your God to the test,'" (Matthew 4:5-7 ESV). Finally, Satan offers Jesus all the kingdoms of the world if He would just fall down and worship him. Jesus this time goes on the offensive, commanding, "Be gone, Satan! For it is written, 'You shall worship the Lord your God and Him only shall you serve,'" (Matthew 4:10 ESV).

Satan is always trying to get in the way but when we wield the power of our God, the enemy is helpless. He's already been defeated by Jesus. We can tap into that power too. Follow Jesus's example and use the Word to ward off Satan's attacks. Remember, he is a liar and is full of deceit. When you feel the Enemy breathing down your neck, recall the words of James 4:7. "Resist the devil and he will flee from you."

BRUCE WAYNE

In 2016 Warner Brothers released a follow-up to Zak Snyder's Superman film *Man of Steel* entitled *Batman v. Superman: Dawn of Justice*. Also directed by Snyder, the film was meant to serve numerous purposes simultaneously. It introduced a new on-screen Batman (played by Ben Affleck), served as a quasi-sequel to *Man of Steel*, introduced Gal Gadot as Wonder Woman, and would set up the eventual *Justice League*. Reaction from both fans and critics have been mixed but one element that was distinctively new to audiences was Affleck's Bruce Wayne.

Heavily drawing inspiration from Frank Miller's *The Dark Knight Returns*, Affleck plays a version of Batman who is much older and worn down from two decades of fighting crime. Disillusioned by losing loved ones and allies, Bruce Wayne has become bitter and resigned to an ongoing fight against crime in Gotham. This bitter version of Batman continues his dual lives with little fulfillment or sense of purpose. Even his victories seem empty as Batman derives little satisfaction from breaking up a human trafficking ring in the film's first act. Batman's disenchantment has even led him to branding criminals with his bat symbol. Bruce Wayne lives in a lake house, which sits near an entrance to the batcave. Wayne Manor is a burnt out husk, having never been repaired following a fire not seen in the film. Alfred seems to be the only person Bruce interacts with on a regular basis.

All of this sets the stage for what eventually becomes Bruce's foremost obsession – defeating Superman. The film retroactively explains that Bruce Wayne was in Metropolis and witnessed firsthand the destruction that was a result of Superman's fight with General Zod (as seen in the climax of *Man of Steel*). Bruce's properties in Metropolis are destroyed, some of his employees seriously injured. He is filled with rage towards this super powered being and decides the only response is a proactive one. Anyone with the potential to level large cities, maybe the entire planet, needs to be stopped at any cost.

This version of Batman is operating solely on anger. The Bible has many passages warning us to be careful with our anger. Proverbs 29:11 (NLT) says, "Fools vent their anger, but the wise quietly hold it back." Batman is so angry and paranoid of Superman that he is played for a fool by Lex Luthor. He becomes a pawn in Luthor's plot to kill Superman, completely unaware of the real threat. Batman is often a character associated with great deductive reasoning but when Superman is suspected to have caused an explosion in Washington DC, Batman snaps. He is blinded by rage and implements a plan to kill the Kryptonian without any investigation.

The Bible warns us not to give into anger so quickly. "Cease from anger, and forsake wrath; do not fret – it only causes harm. For evildoers shall be cut off; but those who wait on the Lord, they shall inherit the earth," Psalms 37:8-9 (NKJV). Don't be so quick to become angry when you're suspicious of someone. First you must get the facts straight and reason calmly with others. Paul warns us in Ephesians 4:26-27 not to let the sun go down while we're still angry.

James 1:19-20 (ESV) says, "Let every person be quick to hear, slow to speak, slow to anger; for the anger of man does not produce the righteousness of God." The impetuous anger of Batman causes much damage, as he and Superman waste crucial time fighting each other instead of stopping Luthor. If you can't properly channel your anger, then it will control you much like Luthor controlled Batman. He nearly kills Superman until he discovers Superman's adoptive mother Martha Kent is being held hostage. The coincidence of Batman's own mother sharing the same name snaps him out of his rage. Batman then goes on to rescue Martha Kent and once again resembles the hero we all know. Paul lists anger amongst negative qualities we must get rid of in Galatians 5:26. If Batman had done so, then Gotham and Metropolis both would have benefited.

Batman: The Return of Bruce Wayne

BATMAN

G rant Morrison is known among Batman fans for having written one of the most ambitious, all-encompassing runs DC has ever published. The centerpiece of this story was "Batman, RIP," published in 2008 in the monthly *Batman*. In the supernatural-tinged arc, Batman battles a cunning new adversary named Dr. Hurt as well as the Joker, and suffers betrayal from a new love interest named Jezebel Jet. The events of the arc dovetail into *Final Crisis,* a crossover event featuring the Justice League fighting against the villainous Darkseid. During this story, Batman is hit by Darkseid's Omega Beams, seemingly killing the Caped Crusader. It is this event that sets up the following mini-series, *The Return of Bruce Wayne.*

The six-parter is both an ode to the genre influences of Batman, such as westerns and detective noir, and also a complicated time travel story. In actuality, Bruce was not killed by Darkseid but instead sent backward in time, to the Stone Age. He has no memory of who he is or how he has been lost in time. Bruce merely has clues to his true identity, such as the remains of his costume and medallions featuring the Superman and Wonder Woman shields. As Bruce moves forward through time, he slowly regains the memory of who he is. When he finally returns to the present, the Justice League are waiting and it isn't a happy reunion.

Darkseid's purpose for not killing Bruce becomes clear. Darkseid has turned Bruce into a ticking time bomb by infecting him with a creature called the Hyper Adaptor, which intends to destroy the known universe, and the JLA must separate it from Bruce's body. They medically stop his heart and Bruce is actually dead for two minutes, during which his life flashes before his eyes. When he is revived, Bruce finally admits what he refers to as the "first truth of Batman, the saving grace." The gunshots that took his parents' lives may have rendered him alone, but he wasn't alone for long. All of his life, Bruce tried to take on his mission by himself, insisting that he was still alone. But after being rescued by his friends Bruce realizes, "I was never alone."

Batman is often portrayed as the ultimate loner hero. One of the major motifs of the character is his seeming preference to work by himself. He is often seen pushing people away. It is a theme that has been touched upon in numerous stories and yet Batman is synonymous with sidekicks and allies, both super powered and non-super powered. However, the final moment of *The Return of Bruce Wayne* may be one of the only places where Batman openly admits and accepts that he's had plenty of help over the years. Alfred Pennyworth, Jim Gordon, Dick Grayson, the Justice League, just to name a few, have all aided and rescued Batman himself.

We sometimes may be tempted to take on a gargantuan task by ourselves. Perhaps it's something at your job, maybe it's raising your kids, a task at your church, or some other burden, but there is likely something that you've been taking on by yourself. We all try to be the loner hero, like Batman for so much of his career. But he isn't alone and neither are we. Besides obviously having God with us wherever we go (Joshua 1:9), He also intended for us to lean on other believers for help as well. Proverbs 27:17 (ESV) says, "Iron sharpens iron and one man sharpens another." Jesus Himself gathered the disciples for the purpose of fellowship with Him and each other.

So when you are overwhelmed with whatever you're battling in life, gather together the members of your own personal Justice League, look to God together as a group, and be victorious!

BATMAN: THE LONG HALLOWEEN

In 1996 and 1997, DC Comics published *Batman: The Long Halloween*, a maxiseries of 14 issues. Written by Jeph Loeb, penciled by Tim Sale, and colored by Gregory Wright, the series instantly become one of the most prestigious Batman stories ever told. It even was amongst the comic books that heavily influenced Christopher Nolan's film trilogy. Taking place in the early days of Batman's career, the story revolves around the efforts of Batman, Harvey Dent, and Jim Gordon to stop a killer nicknamed Holiday. This person commits a heinous crime every holiday and their identity is a mystery throughout the story, even until the end. Holiday is on the loose for a full calendar year, October to October, hence the book's title.

One of the main themes of *The Long Halloween* is what these characters believe in and hold onto in the face of adversity and horror. Holiday truly drives Gotham mad and creates much tension between the city's mafia families and the crazed supervillains of Arkham Asylum. Dent in particular seems to be a target and he is often suspected of actually being Holiday. In the course of investigating these crimes, Dent has acid thrown in his face by Sal Maroni, one of Gotham's most notorious gangsters. As a result, Harvey snaps and becomes Two-Face. It becomes increasingly difficult for Batman and Gordon to hold onto hope throughout these terrible circumstances. Losing Dent as well simply adds to that.

In the final pages of the book, once the Holiday crimes have been stopped, and Two-Face has been incarcerated, Batman and Gordon struggle to find closure. They return to their comfort zones, Gordon at home with his wife and infant son and Batman to Gotham's rooftops. The beginning and the ending of the story are bookended with statements by Bruce Wayne and Batman. Bruce tells someone, "I believe in Gotham City." Batman's closing narration says, "I believe in Batman." These are the things that motivate him to keep going forward with his life despite the difficulties of the past year.

But what about you? What keeps you moving past the pain we all experience? What keeps you motivated beyond the setbacks that we encounter in life? Who do you believe in? If you are a Christian, there can only be one answer – Jesus Christ.

No matter what you face in your life and the failures you've experienced, He will be there to guide you. By believing in Him, you have an impenetrable hope, one that will never fail you. Jesus will never give up on us and will see us through to the end. He is the "author and finisher of our faith" (Hebrews 12:2).

Romans 10:9 (ESV) says, "If you confess with your mouth that Jesus is Lord and believe in your heart that God raised Him from the dead, you will be saved." God has made it simple for us. It is purely a matter of faith and belief.

Utter the words "I believe in Jesus Christ" and you will be saved. Trust in this and bask in the love and protection of the only real Superhero in the universe!

AFTERWORD

How did you enjoy that trip through Gotham? Does it seem like a pretty bleak and hopeless place? It certainly is and its denizens are surely grateful for their watchful protector, their silent guardian, their Dark Knight.

The real world can be just as harsh a place. In fact it often is even worse than the fictional places we read about. However, we have an even greater Hero to depend upon. That Hero is God's only Son, Jesus Christ. The question now becomes, have you put your faith in Him?

Trust in Jesus. He cares for you, He loves you deeply, and He will never leave you. He's the Hero we don't deserve but the one we need. God graciously sacrificed His own son just to save you personally. John 3:16-17 (ESV) says, "For God so loved the world, that He gave His only Son, that whoever believes in Him should not perish but have eternal life. For God did not send His Son into the world to condemn the world, but in order that the world might be saved through Him."

Let Jesus into your life and let Him make it new. Then the next time you find yourself enjoying the latest adventure featuring the Dark Knight, allow your mind to see the real Hero's reflection and thank God for Him!

REFERENCES

Burton, Tim, director. *Batman.* Warner Brothers, 1989.

Burton, Tim, director. *Batman Returns.* Warner Brothers, 1992.

Dixon, Chuck. *Batman: Vengeance of Bane.* DC Comics, 1993.

Dixon, Chuck. *Robin II: The Joker's Wild.* DC Comics, 1991.

"Heart of Ice." *Batman: The Animated Series*, written by Paul Dini, directed by Bruce Timm, Warner Brothers, 1992.

"His Silicon Soul." *Batman: The Animated Series,* written by Marty Isenberg and Robert N. Skir, directed by Boyd Kirkland, Warner Brothers, 1992.

Hill, Sefton, Rocksteady Studios. *Batman: Arkham Knight.* Warner Brothers, 2014. PlayStation 4.

"I am the Night." *Batman: The Animated Series,* written by Michael Reaves, directed by Boyd Kirkland, Warner Brothers, 1992.

"It's Never Too Late." *Batman: The Animated Series*, written by Tom Ruegger, directed by Boyd Kirkland, Warner Brothers, 1992.

"Joker's Favor." *Batman: The Animated Series,* written by Paul Dini, directed by Boyd Kirkland, Warner Brothers, 1992.

Kirkland, Boyd, director. *Batman & Mr. Freeze: SubZero.* Warner Brothers 1998.

Loeb, Jeph. *Batman: The Long Halloween.* DC Comics, 1996-1997.

"Mad as a Hatter." *Batman: The Animated Series,* written by Paul
Dini, directed by Frank Paur, Warner, Brothers, 1992.

"Mad Love." *The New Batman Adventures,* written by Paul Dini,
story by Paul Dini and Bruce Timm, directed by Butch Lukic,
Warner Brothers, 1999.

Morrison, Grant. *Batman: The Return of Bruce Wayne.*
DC Comics, 2010.

Nolan, Christopher, director. *Batman Begins.* Warner Brothers, 2005.

Nolan, Christopher, director. *The Dark Knight.*
Warner Brothers, 2008.

Nolan, Christopher, director. *The Dark Knight Rises.* Warner
Brothers, 2012.

"Nothing to Fear." *Batman: The Animated Series,* written by Henry
Gilroy and Sean Catherine Derek, directed by Boyd Kirkland,
Warner Brothers 1992.

O'Neil, Dennis. Afterword. *Batman: Knightfall, A Novel.* New York:
Bantam Books. 1994.

"Pretty Poison." *Batman: The Animated Series,* written by Tom
Ruegger, story by Paul Dini and Michael Reaves, directed by
Boyd Kirkland, Warner Brothers, 1992.

Radomski, Eric. Timm, Bruce, directors. *Batman: Mask of the
Phantasm.* Warner Brothers 1993.

"Robin's Reckoning: Part I." *Batman: The Animated Series,* written by
Randy Rogel, directed by Dick Sebast, Warner Brothers, 1993.

"Robin's Reckoning: Part II." *Batman: The Animated Series,* written by
Randy Rogel, directed by Dick Sebast, Warner Brothers, 1993.

Snyder, Zack, director. *Batman v. Superman: Dawn of Justice.*
Warner Brothers, 2016.

The Holy Bible. English Standard Version, Crossway Bibles, 2001.

The Holy Bible. New International Version, Zondervan, 1973.

The Holy Bible. New King James Version, 1982.

The Holy Bible. New Living Translation, 1996.

"The Underdwellers." *Batman: The Animated Series,* written by Tom Ruegger, directed by Frank Paur, Warner Brothers, 1992.

"Two-Face Part I." *Batman: The Animated Series,* story by Alan Burnett, teleplay by Randy Rogel, directed by Kevin Altieri, Warner Brothers, 1992.

"Two-Face Part II." *Batman: The Animated Series,* written by Randy Rogel, directed by Kevin Altieri, Warner Brothers, 1992.